The Minimalist Coloring Book

The Absence of Coloring Contains All Coloring
—Zen Koan

by Craig Conley

High Brow Pencil Press
DURHAM, NC

All colors tend to white,
the fiercer the intensity of light
—Marcel Minnaert

Within the very sunlight are all the colors of white,
the pure chaos from which springs all life.
—L. E. Modesitt Jr.

White still outsells all other paint colors
by a huge margin.
—Susan Sargent

INTRODUCTION

This coloring book contains images of white things, printed on white paper. Is one to fill in these images with a white crayon? Or is one to let go of the crayon and practice the Taoist concept of wu-wei (actionless action)?

Why color white objects white?

◊ White is the absence of color which contains all colors.

◊ It's easy to keep within the lines.

◊ It helps one to focus on process, not results.

◊ It fulfills Zen Master Han-Shan's invitation to "leap the world's ties and sit among the white clouds."

◊ It is a rejection of artifice, an unveiling of the void.

◊ It is an antidote to art theory.

Why not color white objects white?

◊ In Zen terms, the absence of coloring contains all coloring.

PICKET FENCE

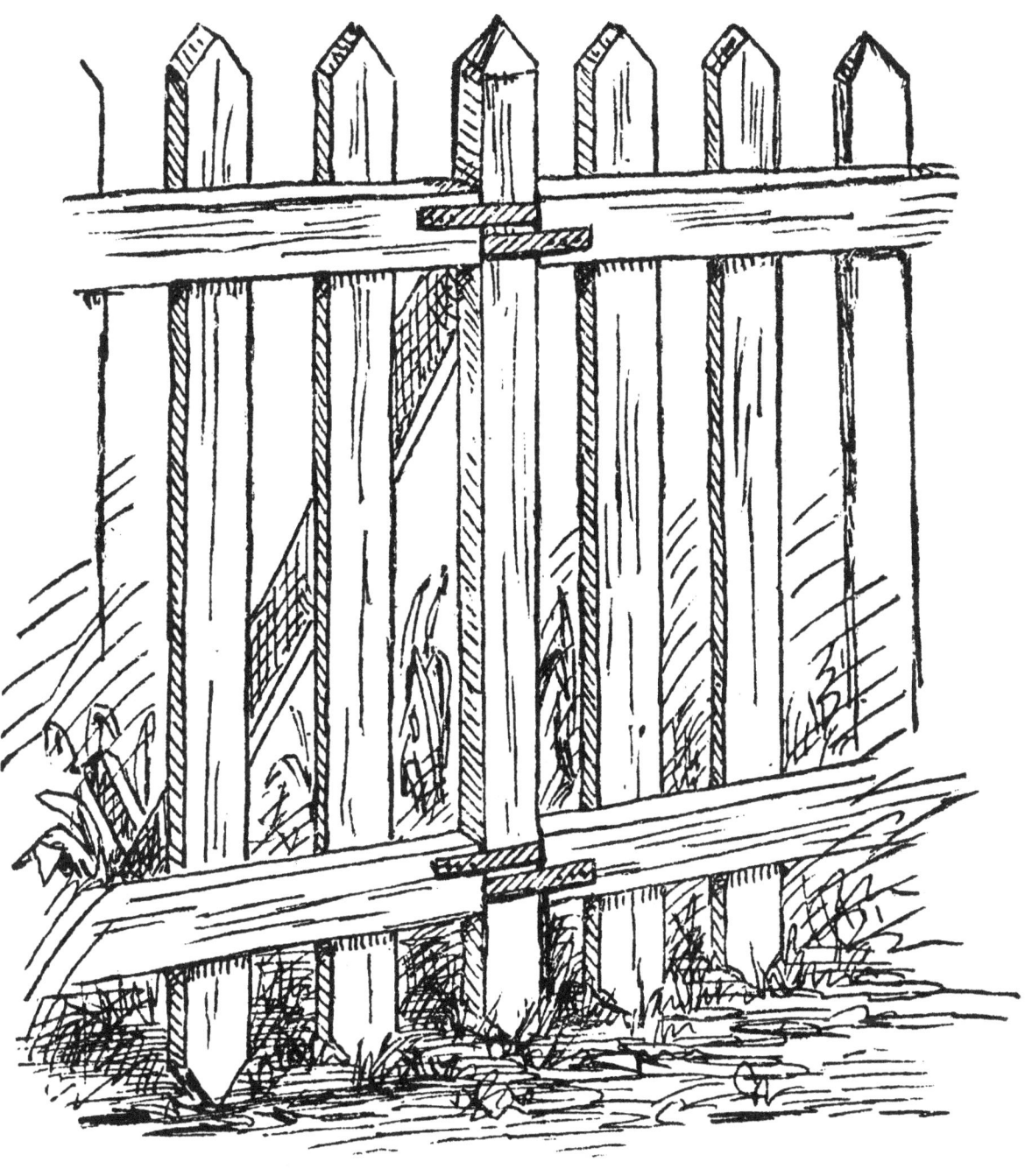

The picket fence was as white as the snow that had not yet fallen. —W.D. Valgardson, *Red Dust* (1978)

FINE CHINA

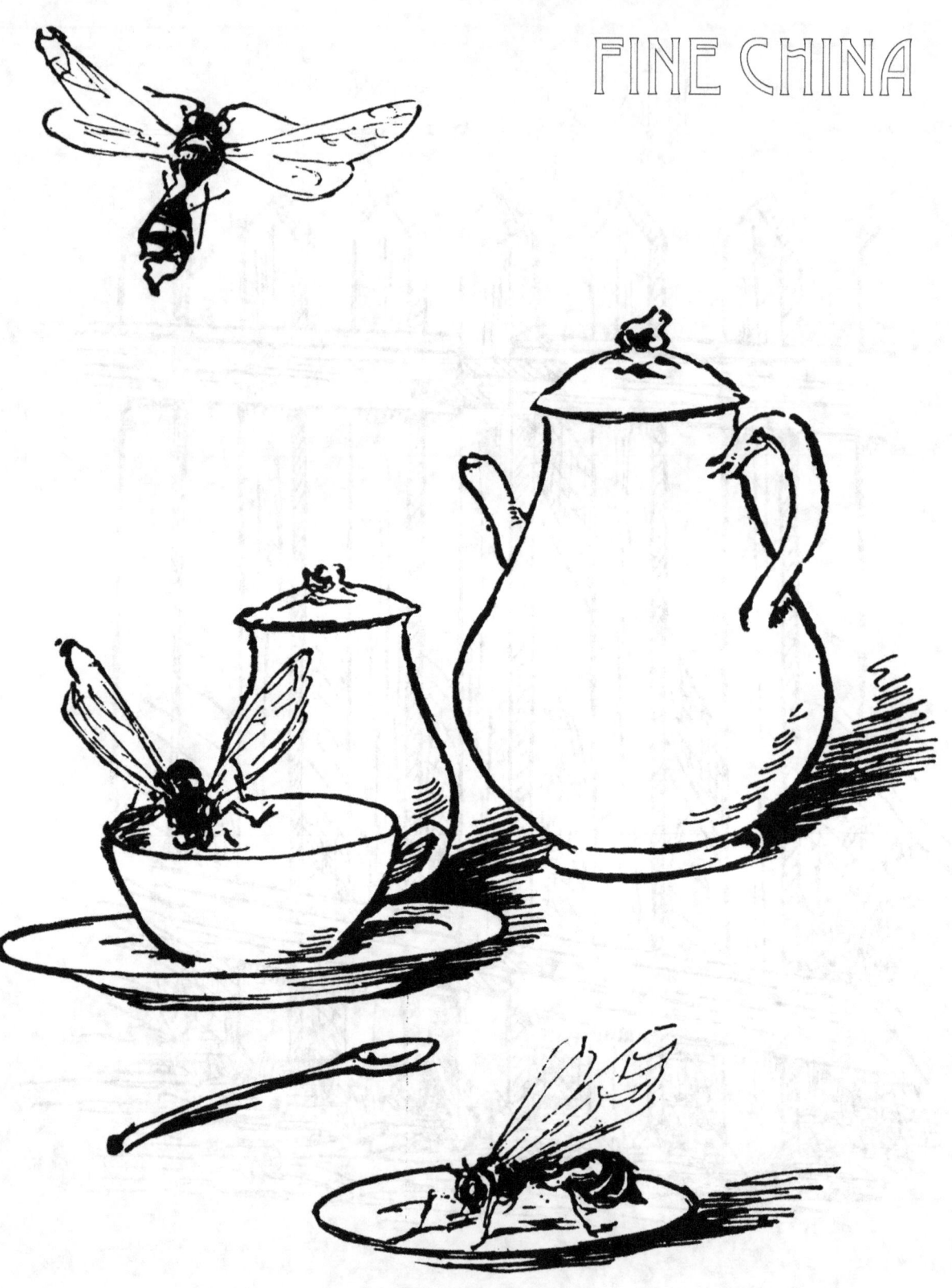

His mother was sitting down, her face as white as the bone china cup she was holding.
—Sidney L. Dornfest, *The Pincus Legacy* (2005)

SNOWMAN

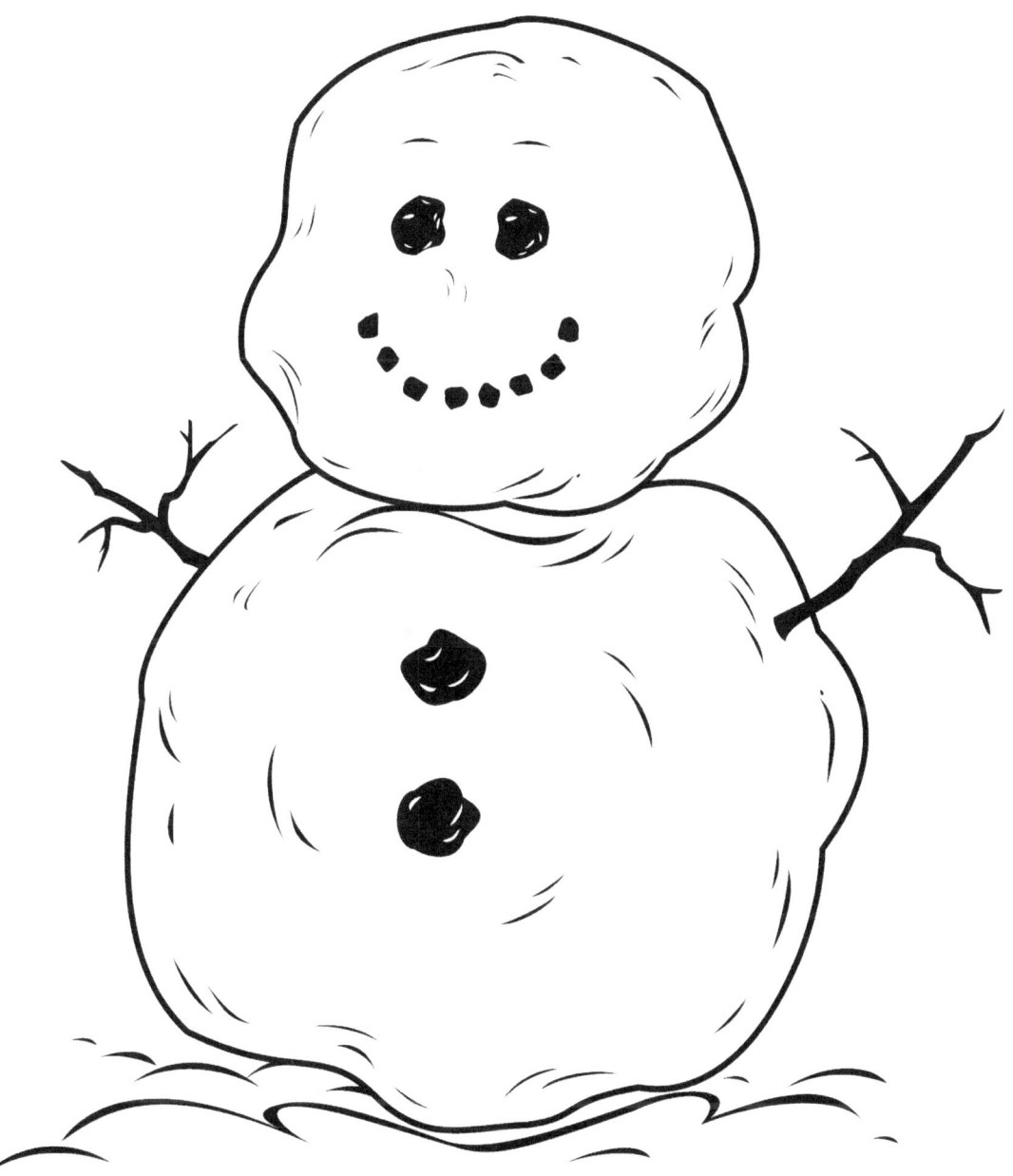

Hui and I chased the snow with our eyes closed and arms outstretched. The earth seemed to be rising upward as the snowy butterflies fell gracefully. Hui stood silently still with snow dusting him and sliding down his slender fingers. Soon he was white as a snowman. In this swirling white silk, I held my heart in my hands, confessing my love for this northern wintry tale. In this perfect world, I also became a snowman.

—Da Chen, *Sounds of the River* (2002)

MUMMY

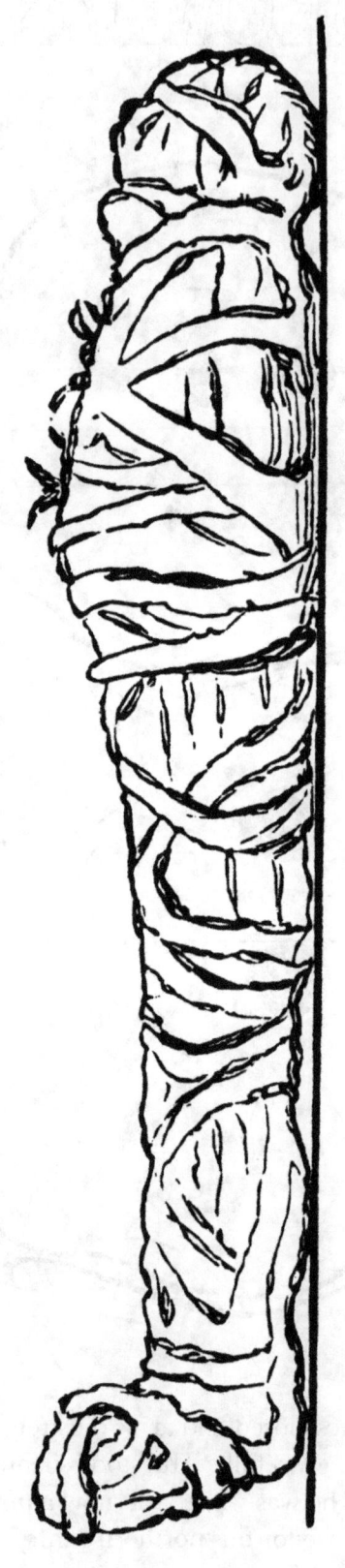

The dust lay dead and white
As powder on a mummy's face
—Dame Edith Sitwell, "Clowns' Houses" (1918)

SUGAR CUBE

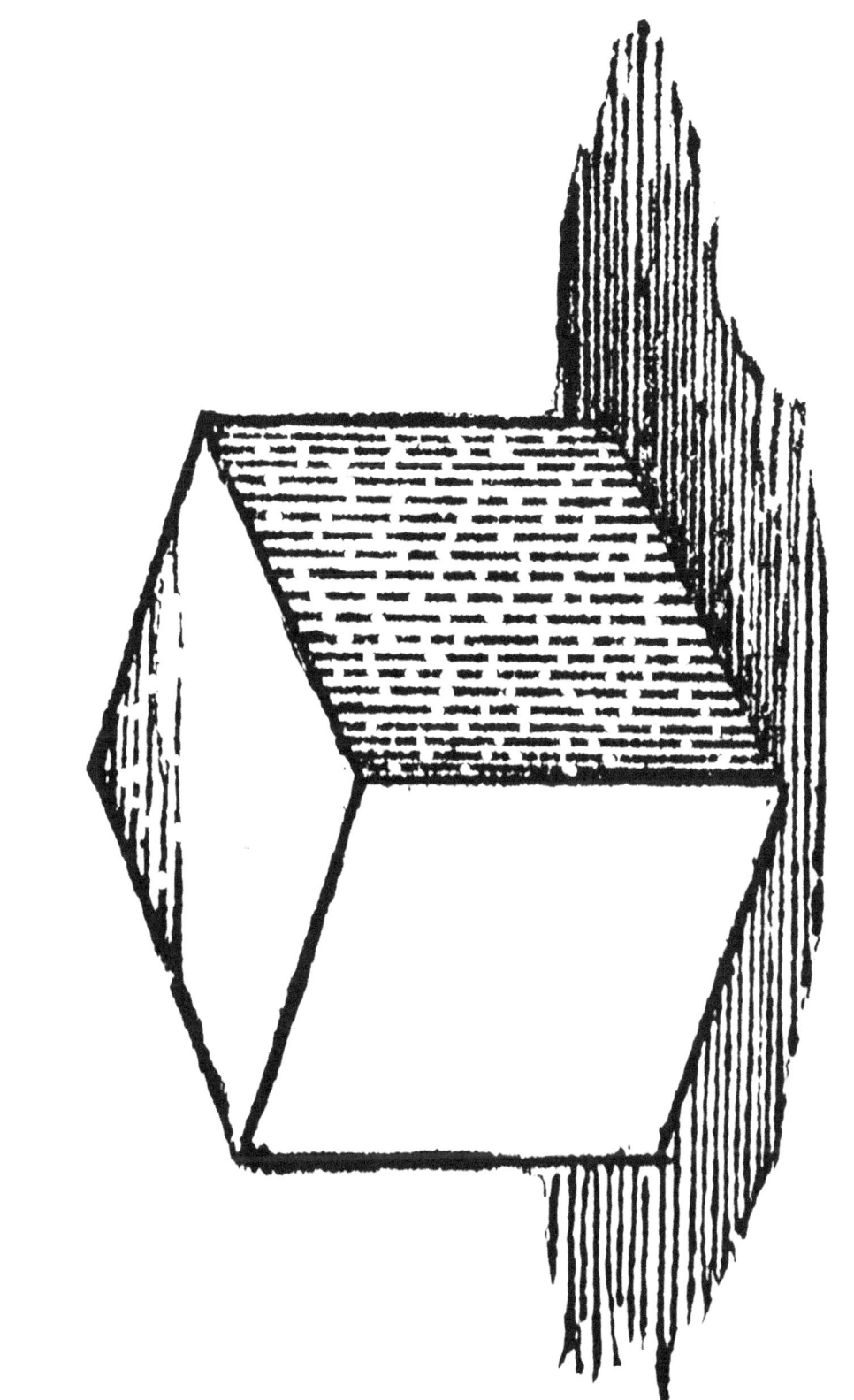

But don't say my precious little sugar cube is like an animal. She has a soul, a soul washed white as the cleanest sheet by the holy waters of Baptism. —*Partisan Review & Anvil*, vol. 3 (1935)

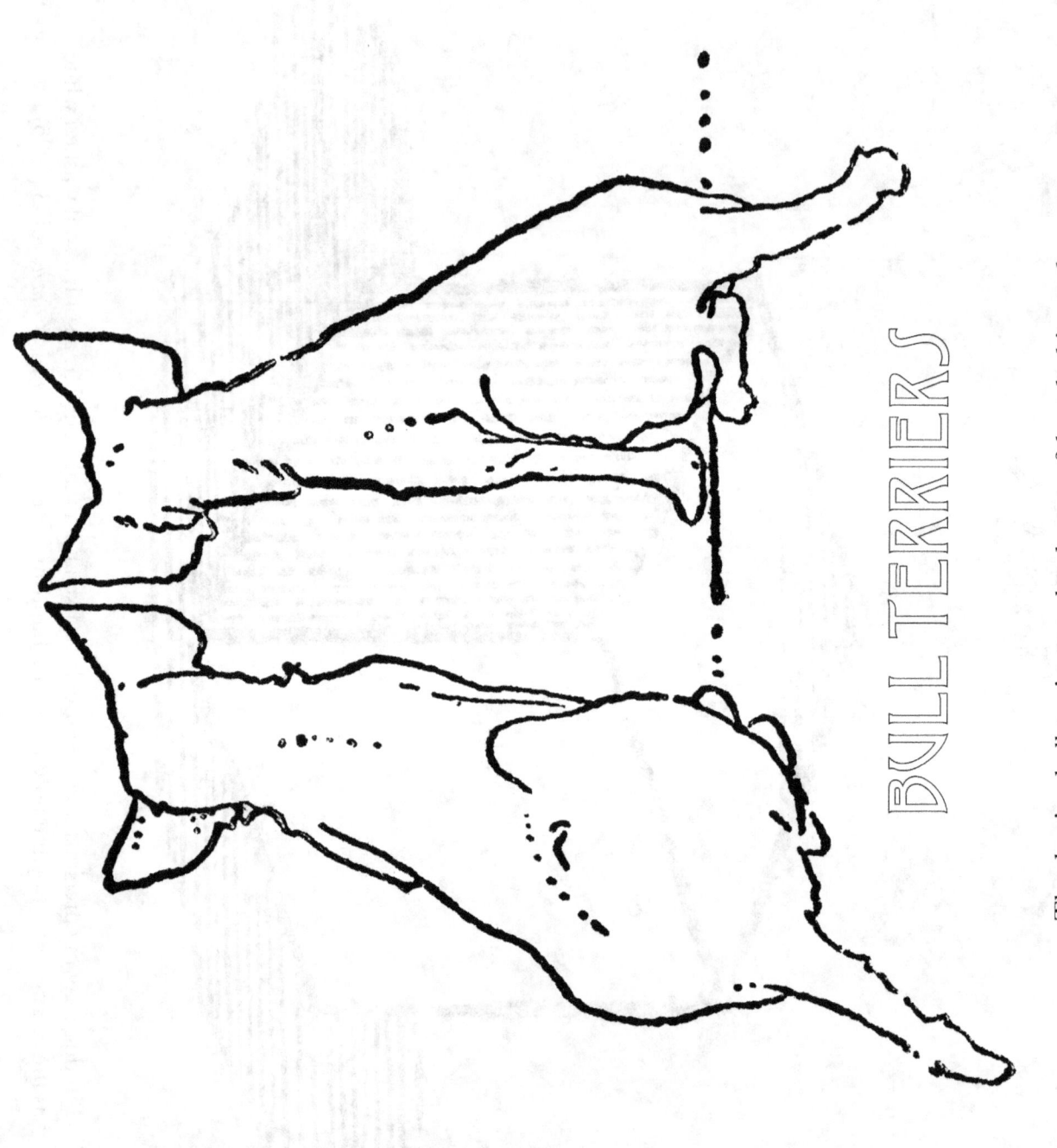

BULL TERRIERS

The dog is a bull terrier, purebred, powerful, and white as the shell sand on the beach. —Baker Brownell, *Art Is Action* (1969)

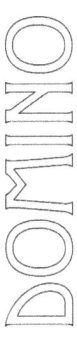

DOMINO

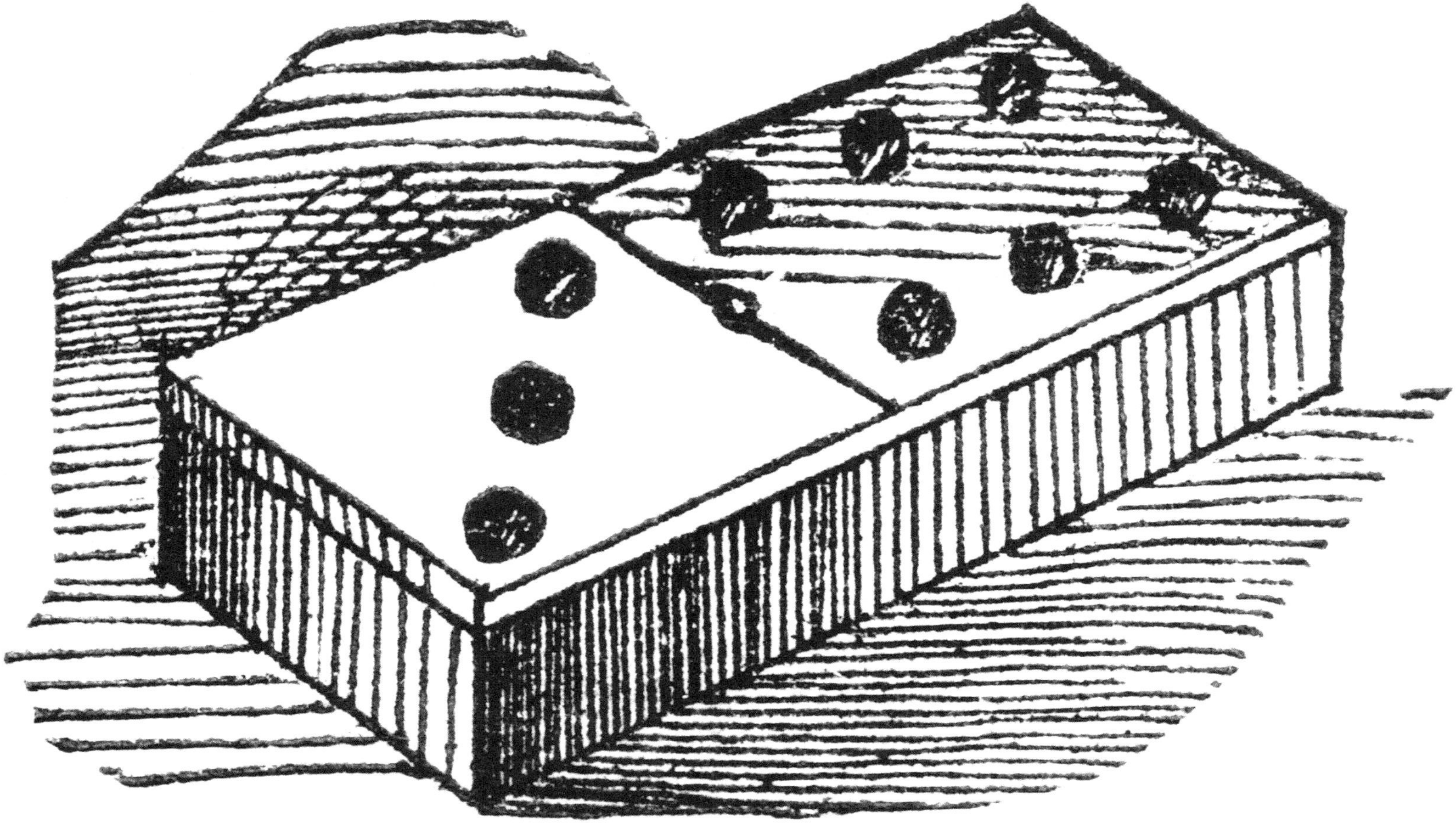

White dominoes, set and ready to tumble in the long white room. —Al Compton, *Carve the Ivory* (2001)

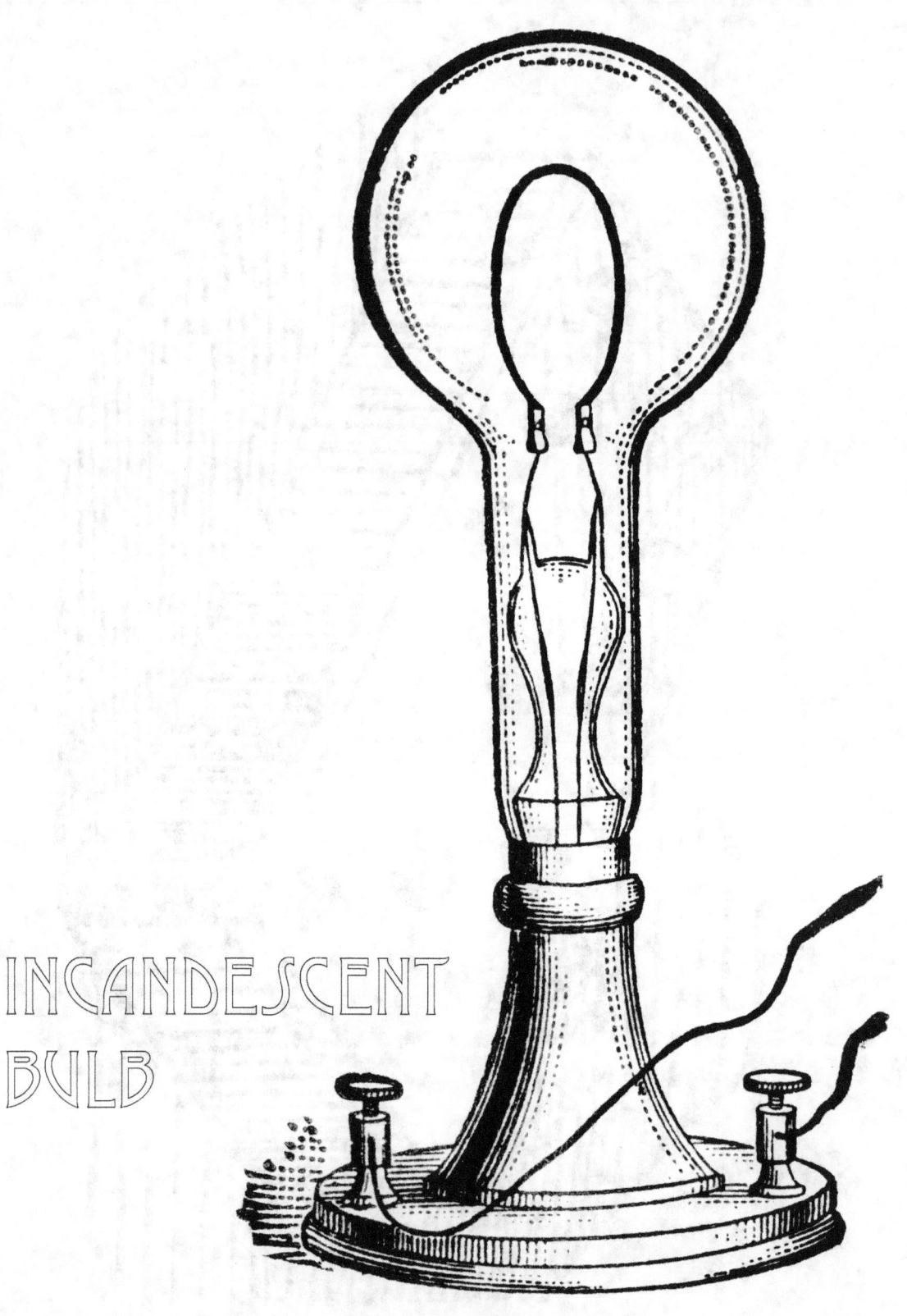

INCANDESCENT
BULB

The bright light bulbs, white as sugar, flashed on, lighting up vast maps of the Crimea.
—Osip Mandelstam, *Theodosia* (1985)

DOVE OF PEACE

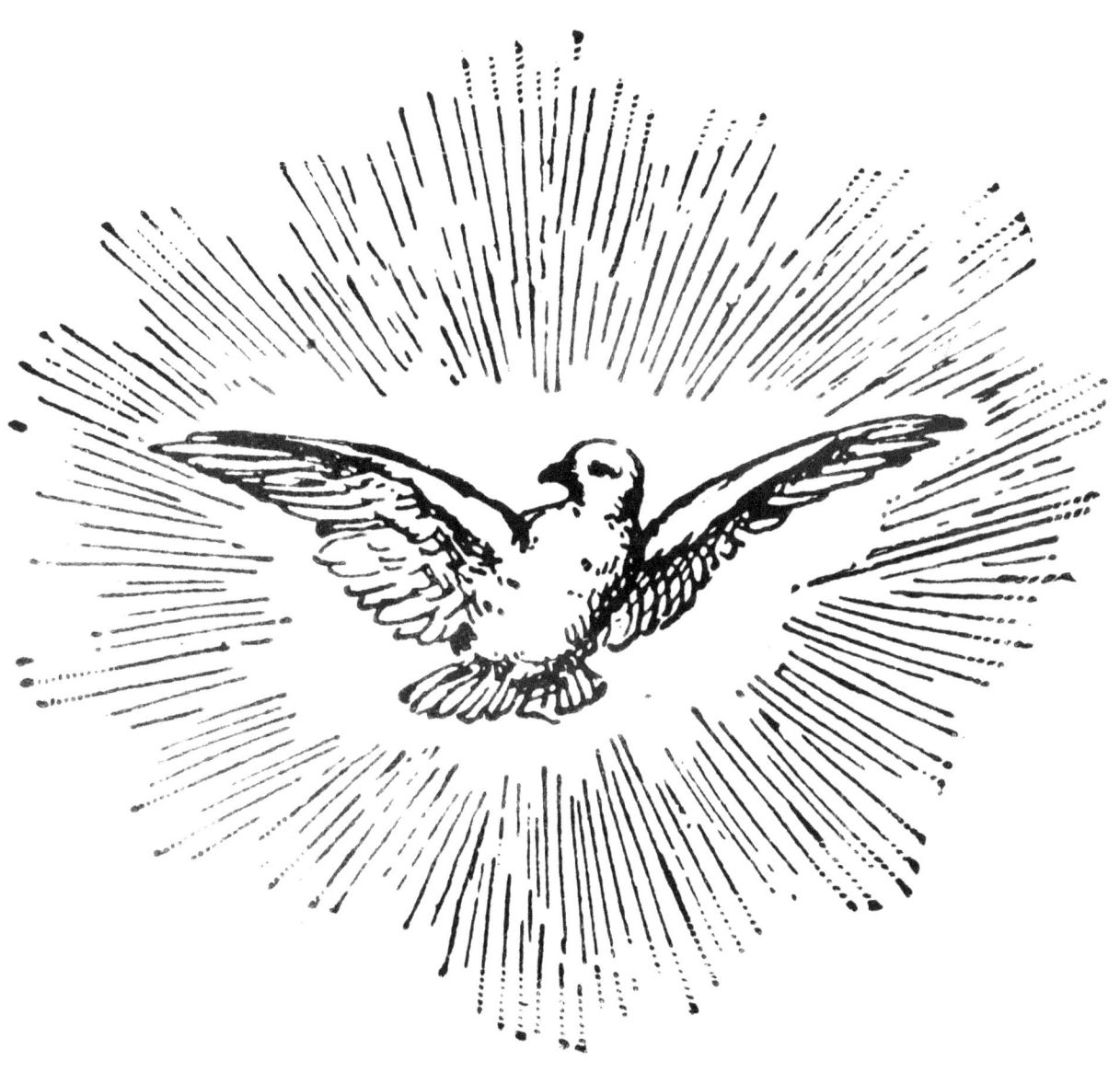

And in the vastness of her loneliness a pure joy flew, white as a dove.
—Niall Williams, *As It Is in Heaven* (1999)

WHITE ROSE

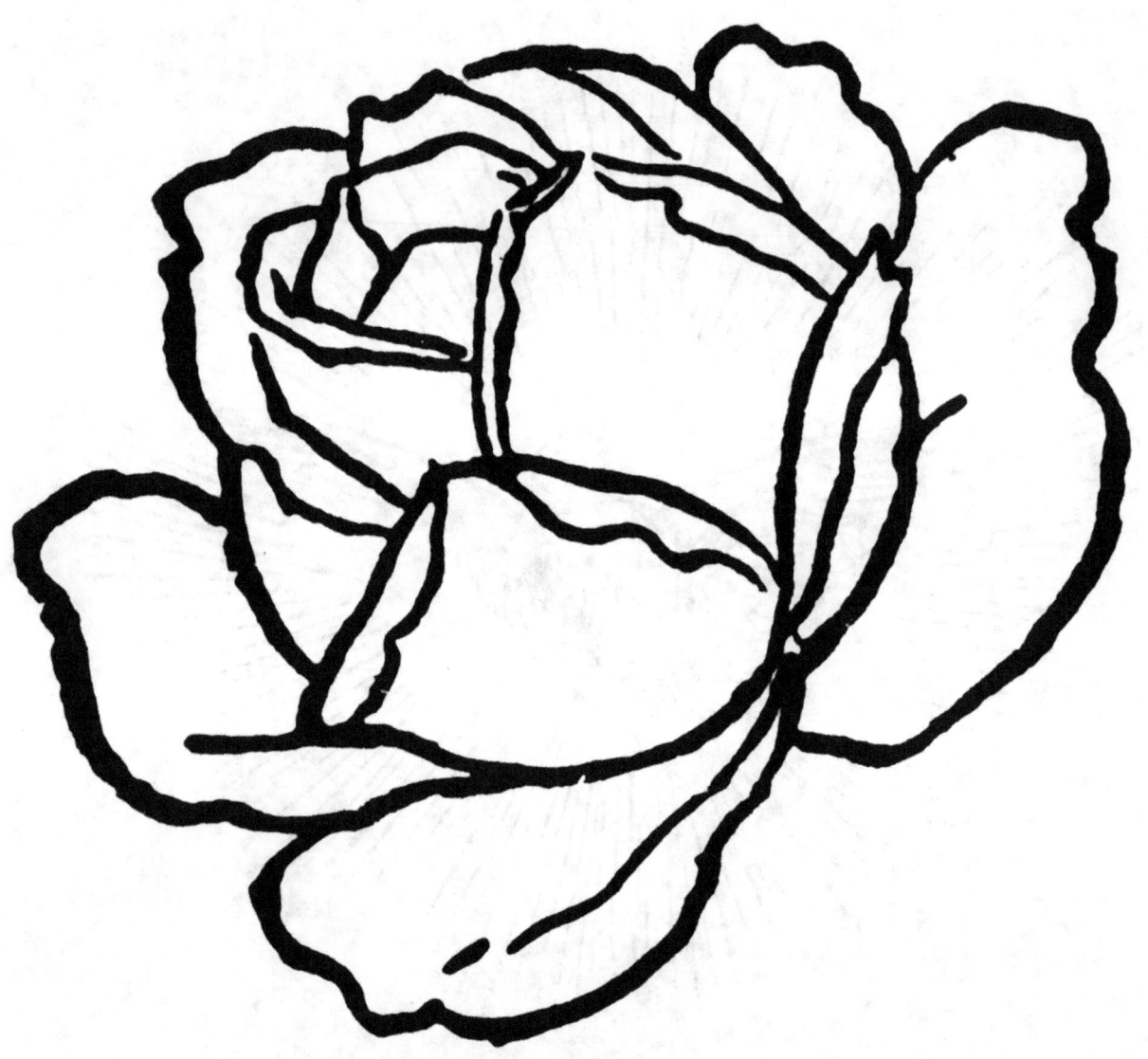

My roses are white, as white as the foam of the sea, and whiter than the snow upon the mountain.
—Oscar Wilde, *The Happy Prince* (1888)

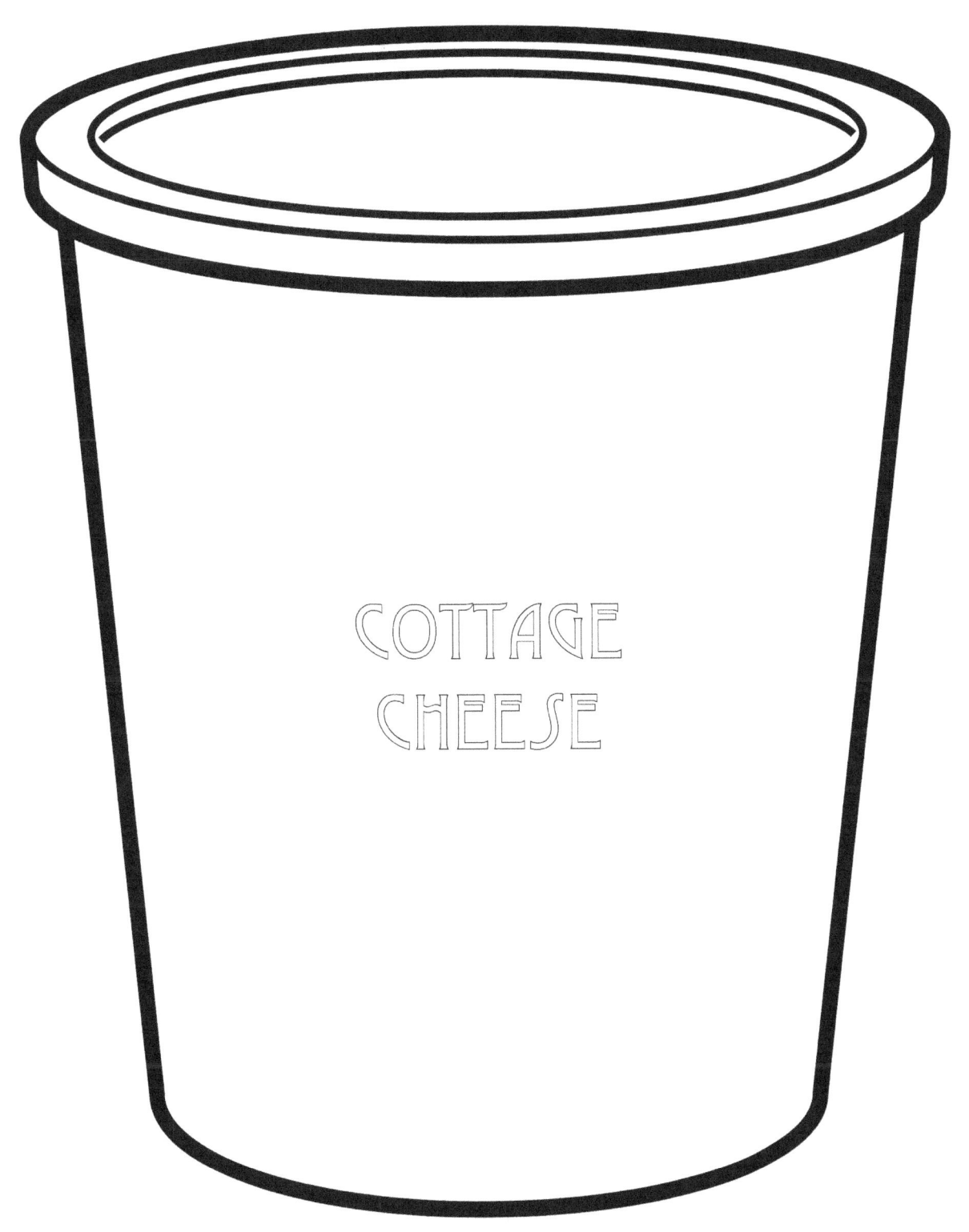

COTTAGE
CHEESE

Harriet came out in the whitest of white dresses, carrying a tray with . . . butter and milk and cottage cheese.
—David Grayson, "The Celebrity," *The American Magazine* (1910)

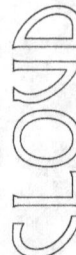

CLOUD

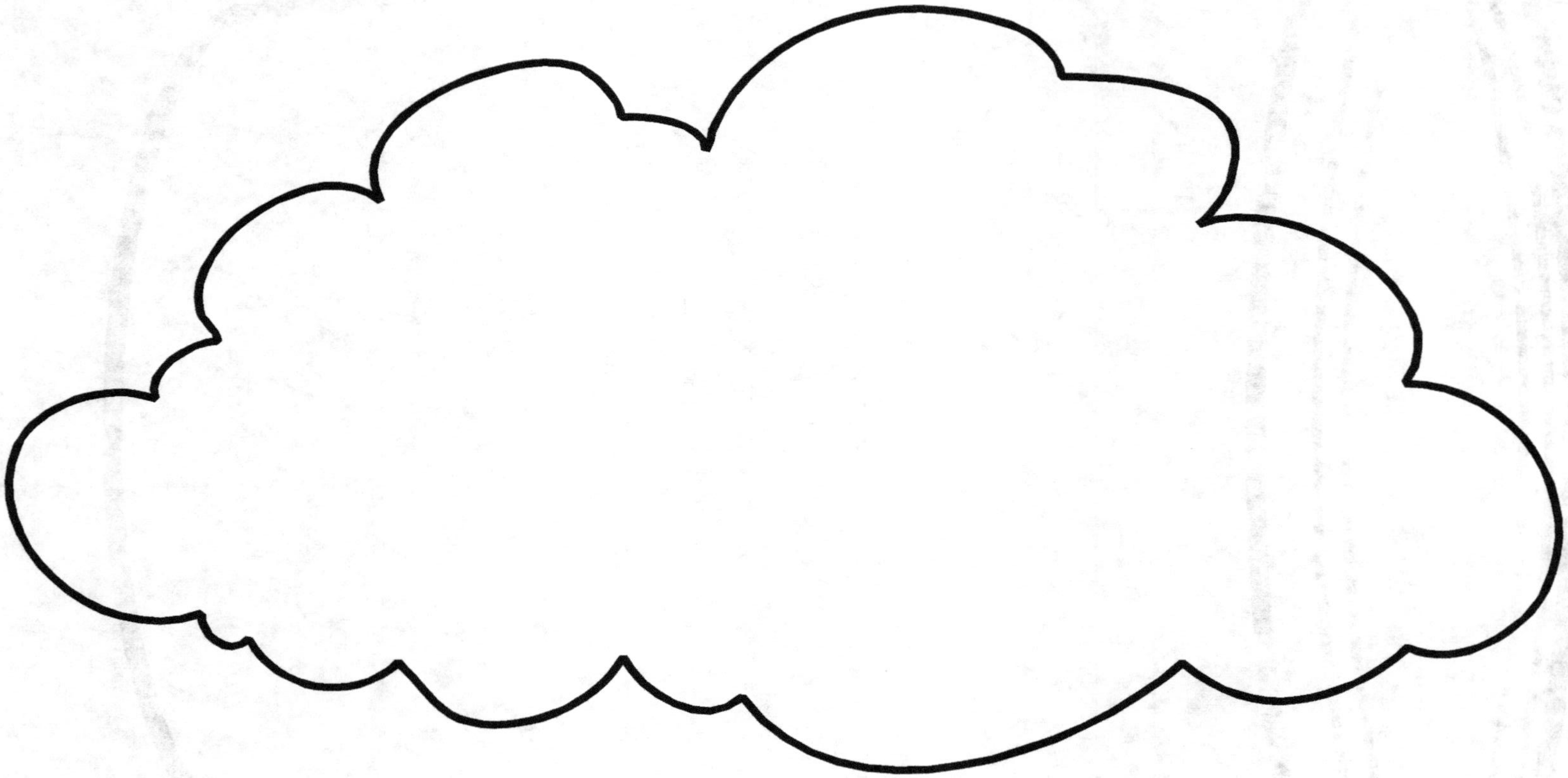

A massive cloud of pure pearl luster, apparently as fixed and calm as the meadows and groves in the shadow beneath it, was arched across the Valley from wall to wall, one end resting on the grand abutment of El Capitan, the other on Cathedral Rock.

—John Muir, *The Yosemite* (1912)

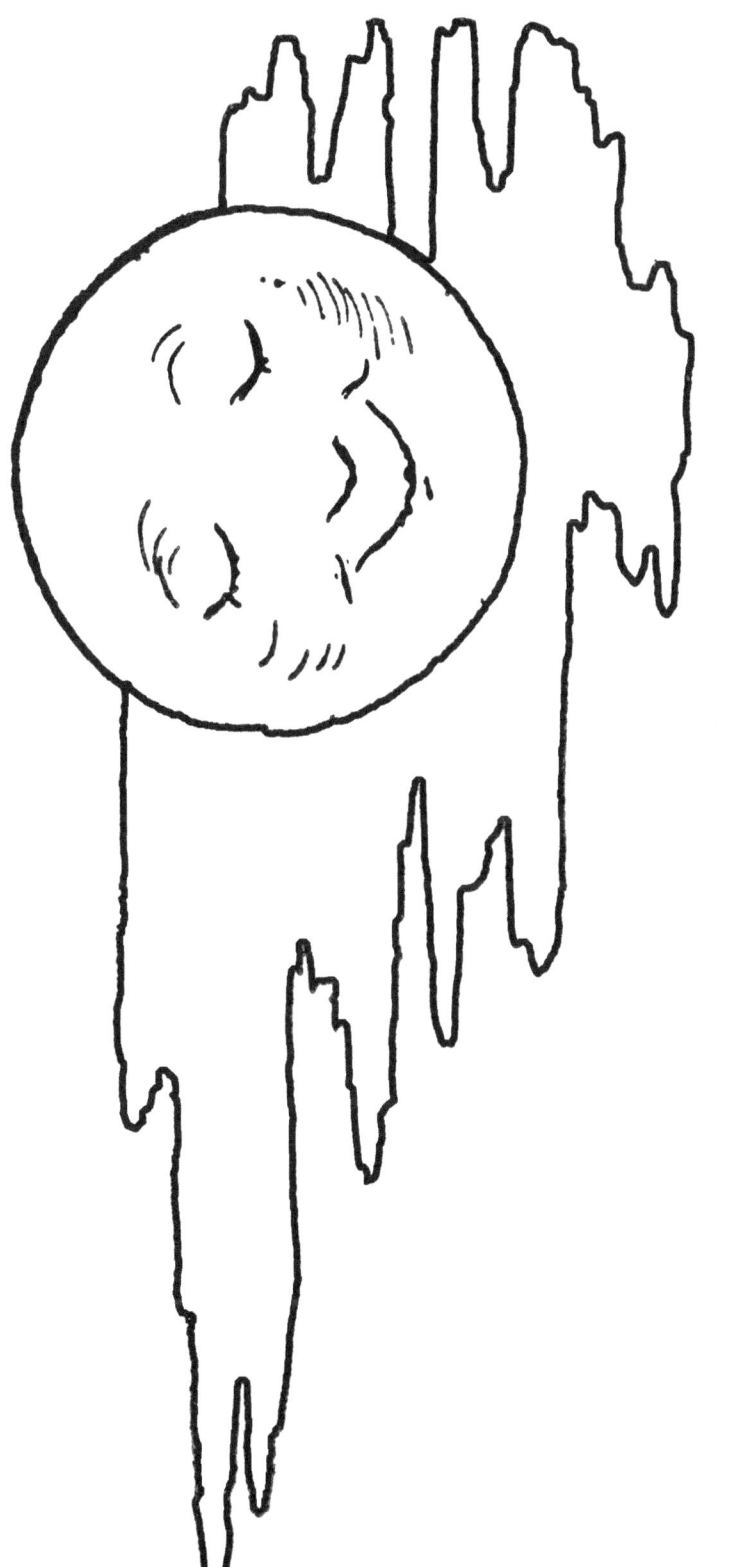

One night, under a full moon, the egg opened and a strange bird was born.

—Thich Nhat Hahn, *Love in Action* (1993)

FULL MOON

WHITE OWL

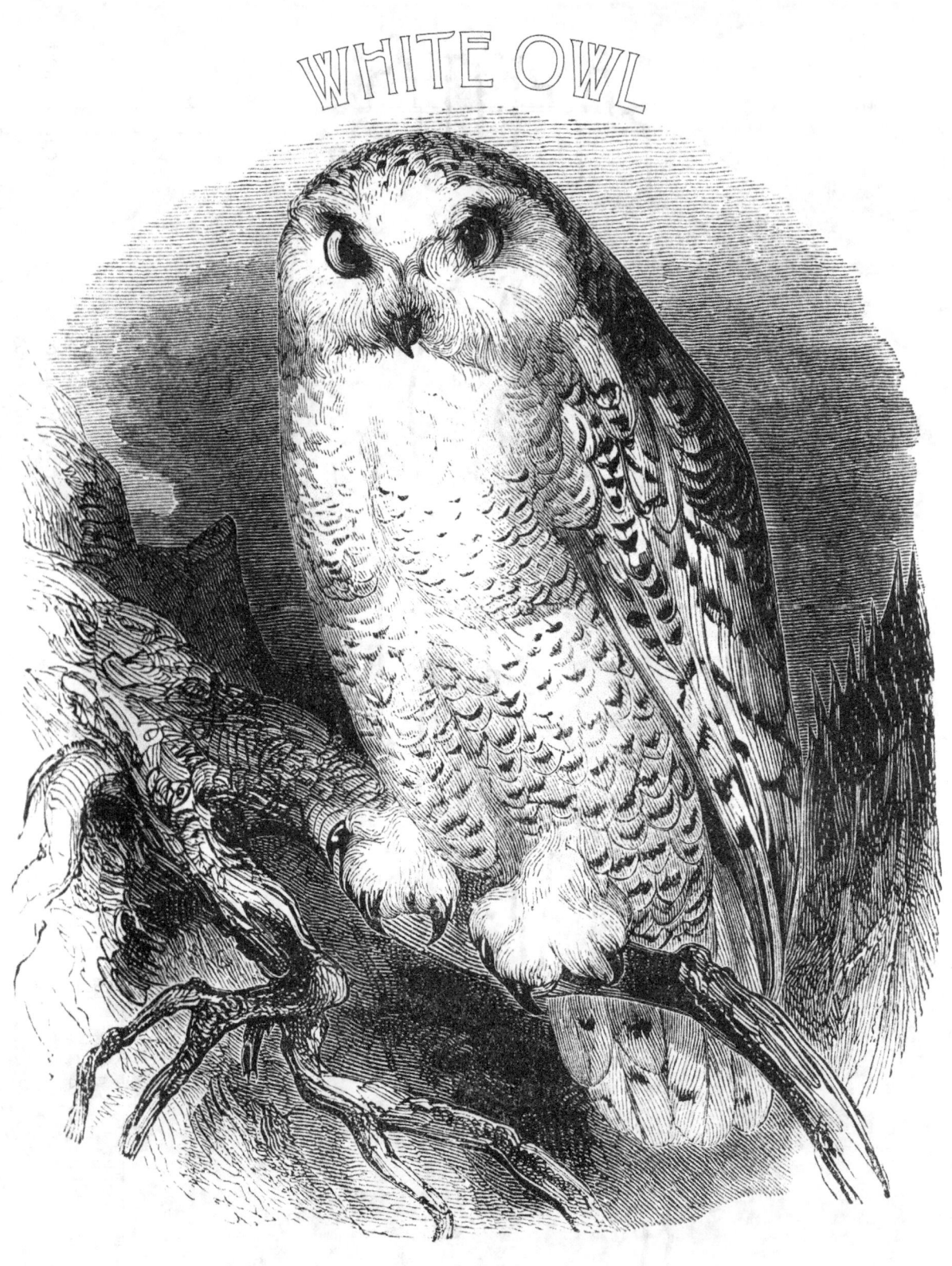

That night, a white owl appeared to his grandmother as she dreamed.
—Joseph Bruchac, *Return of the Sun* (1990)

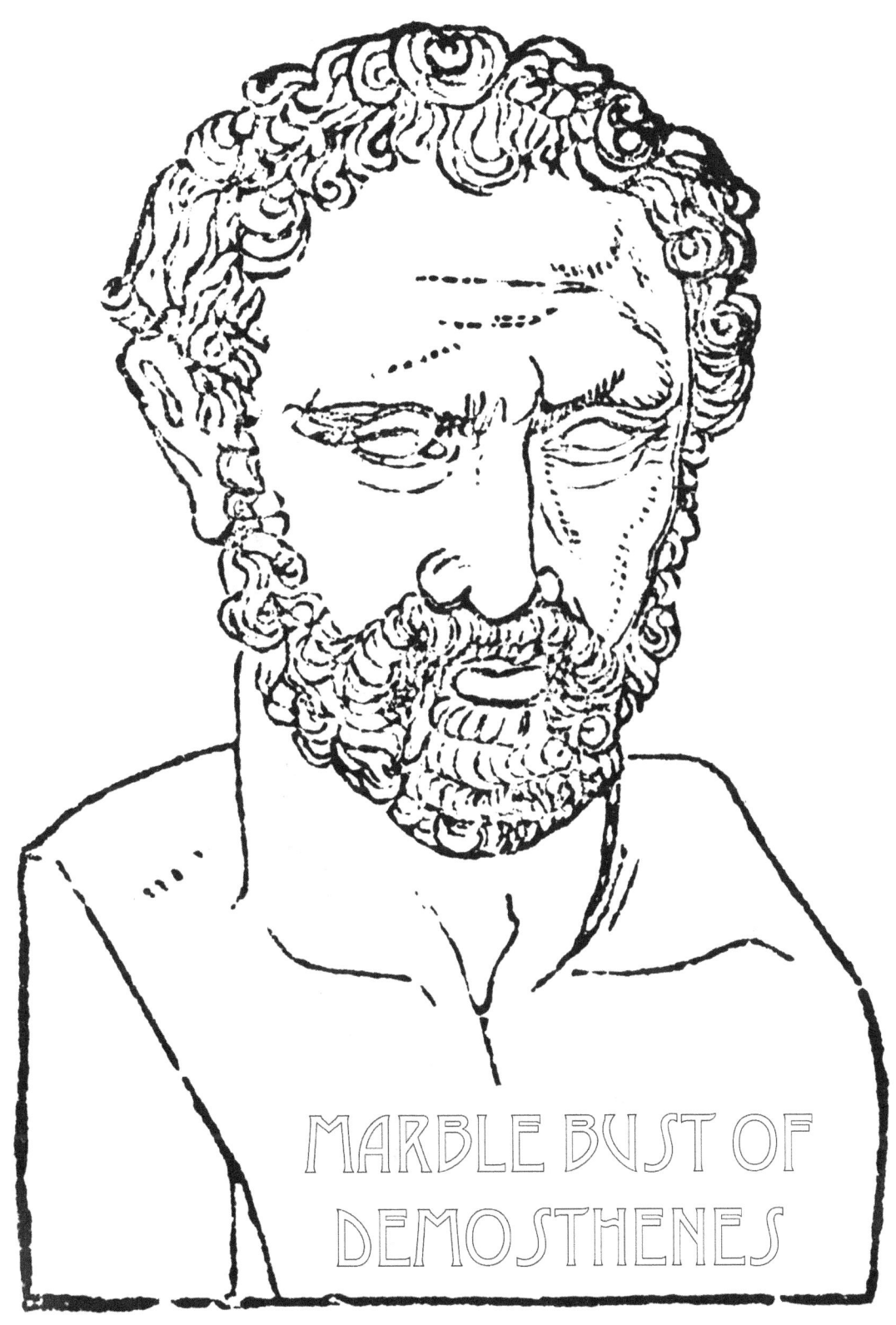

MARBLE BUST OF
DEMOSTHENES

Ernest looked like a marble bust of himself.
—Inez Haynes Gillmore, "Till He Gets Him a Wife," *The American Magazine* (1912)

HEN'S EGG

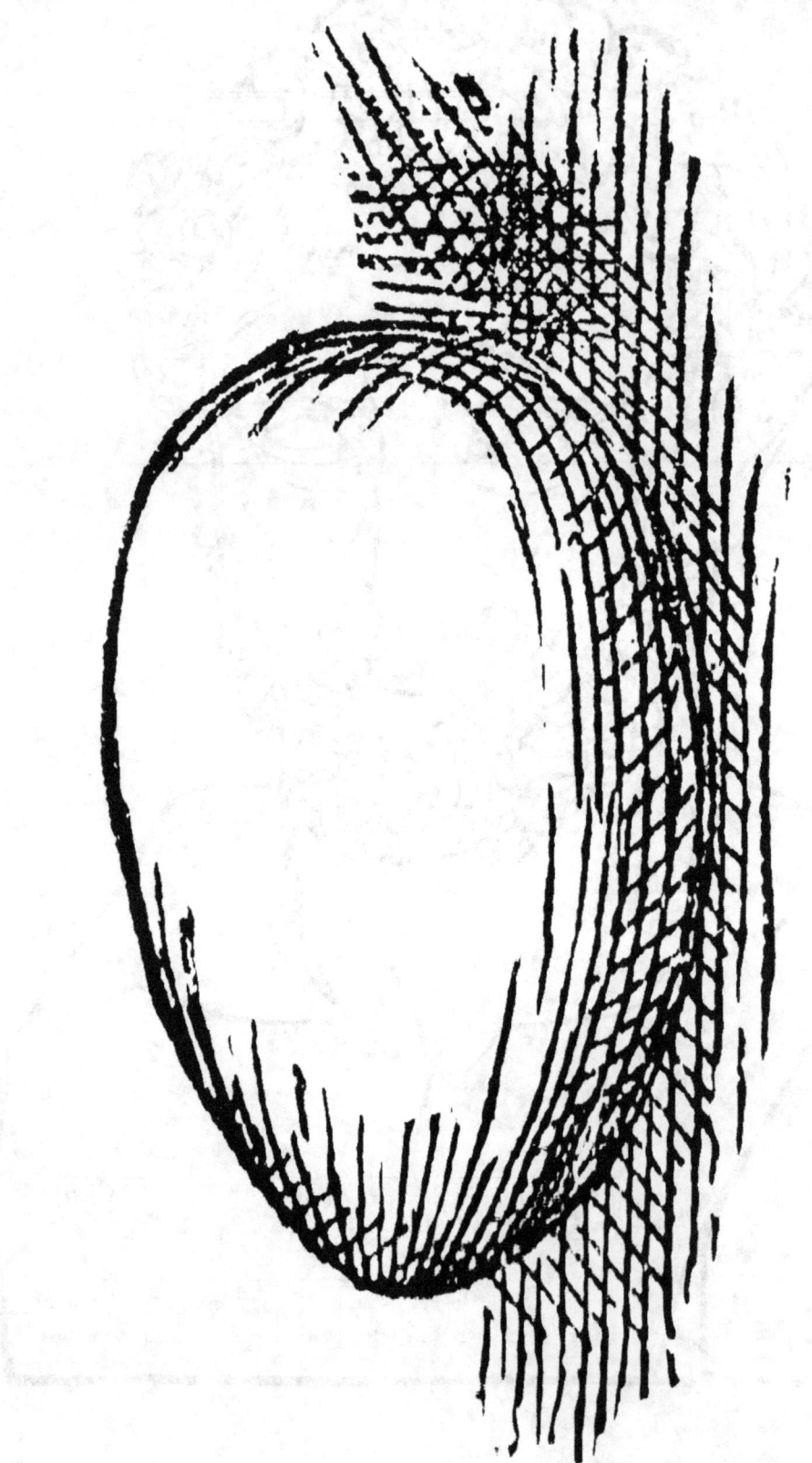

He appeared as the clown once more, his face white as an egg.
—Padraic Colum, *Half-Day's Ride* (1932)

WHITE CLIFFS
OF DOVER

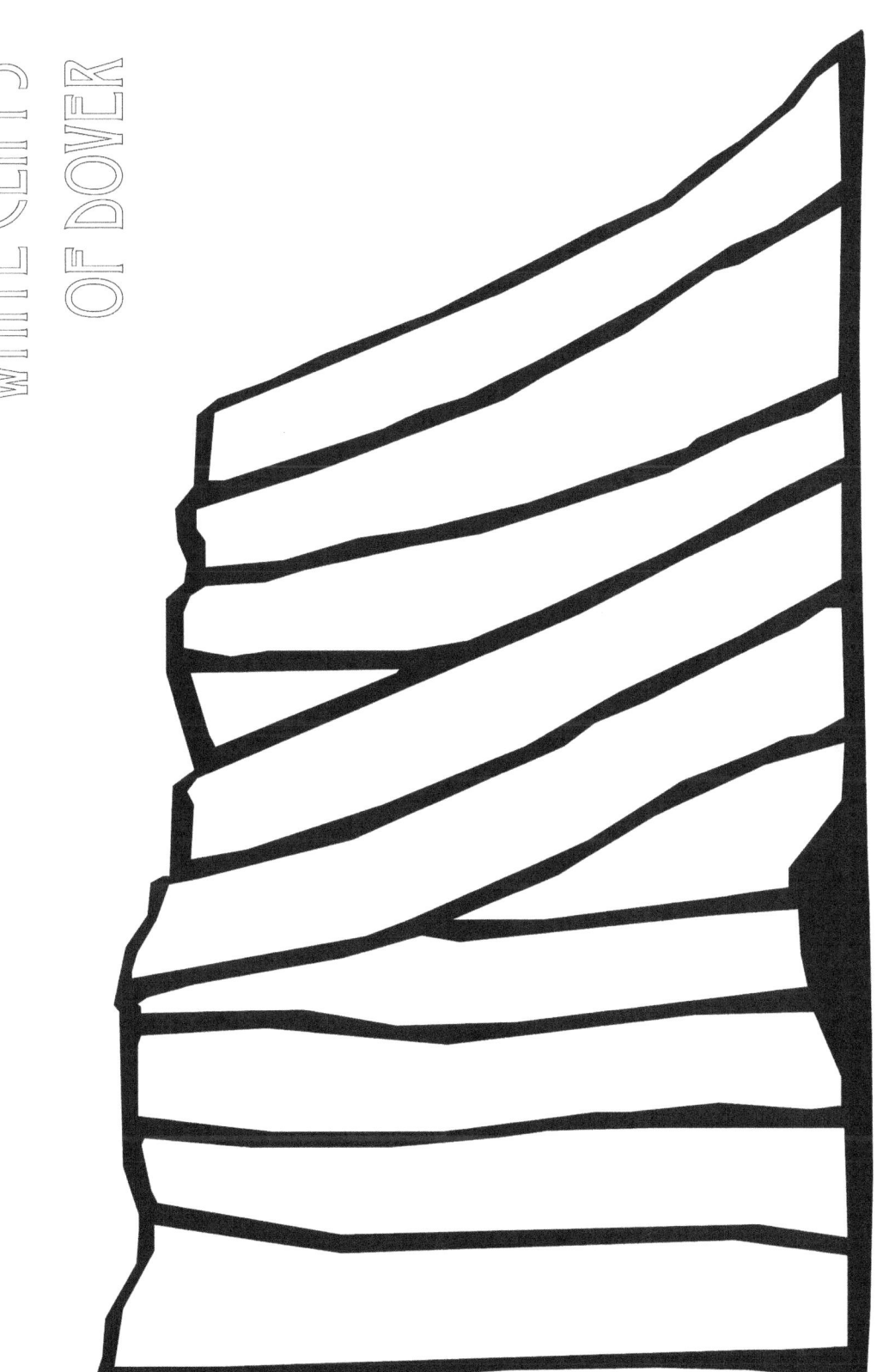

The cliffs of Dover sprang from the loamy coast as if planted from Olympian seed—a cloud-high treacherous wall of undulating oyster-colored rock. The Almighty's wondrous sculpture, blinding white as it reflected the rays of midday sun.

—Faye Kellerman, *The Quality of Mercy* (2002)

SAND DOLLAR

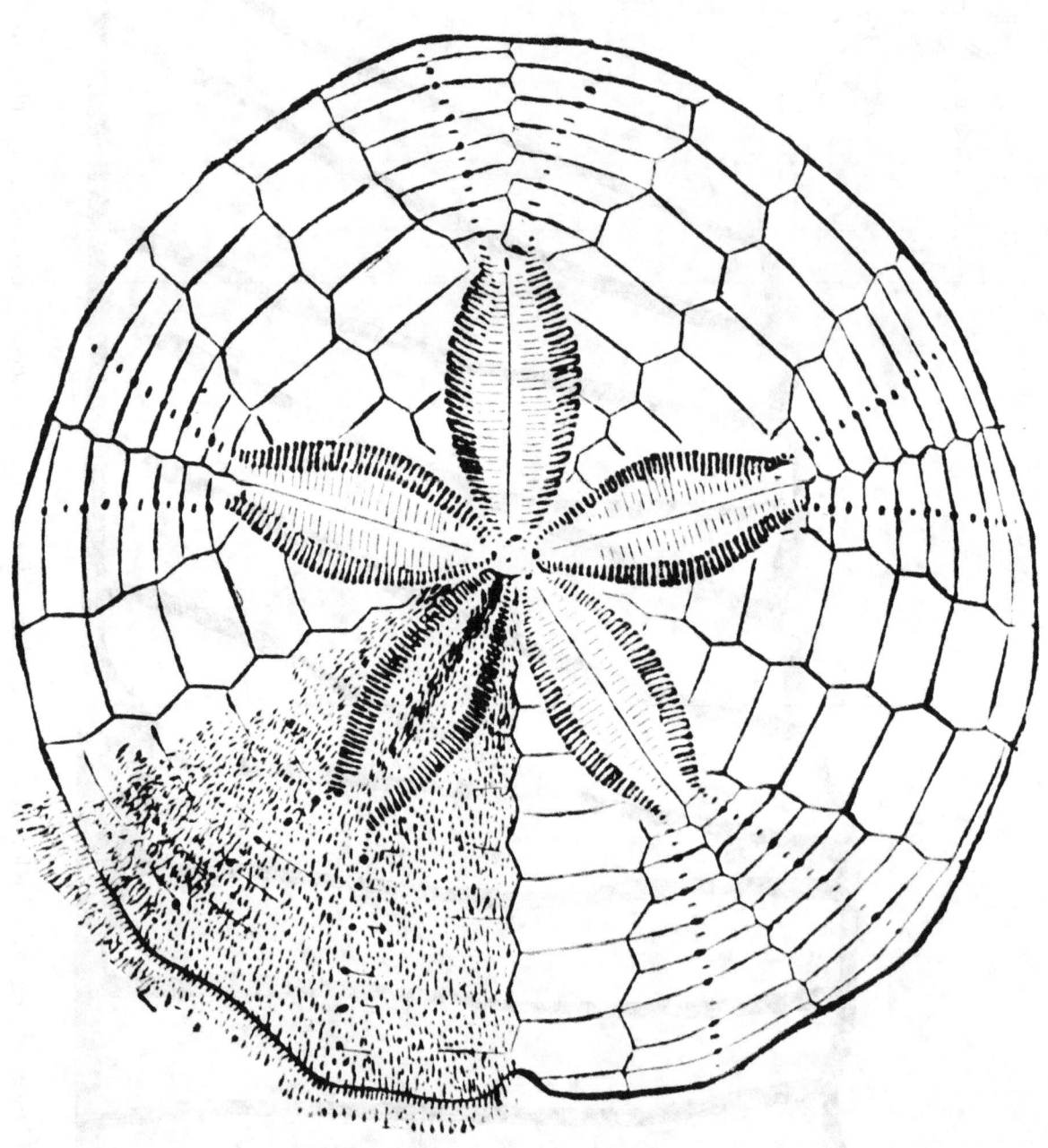

He bent and pocketed the handsome, white-bleached sand dollar he'd placed in the tower early that morning.
—Carole S. Adler, *The Magic of the Glits* (1979)

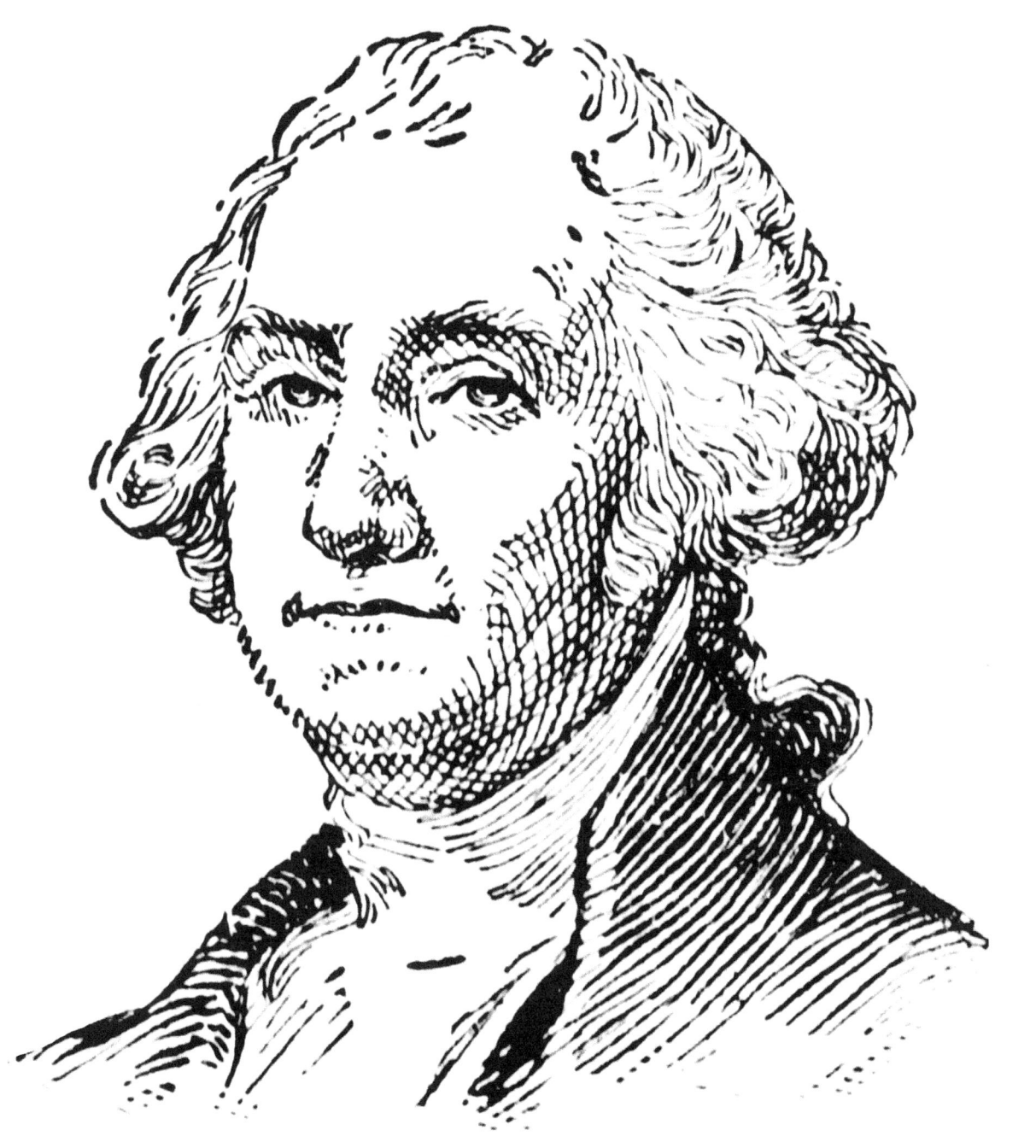

GEORGE WASHINGTON

He wore a powdered wig after the fashion of the times.
—*The Christian's Penny Magazine* (1865)

FLOUR MOTH'S WING

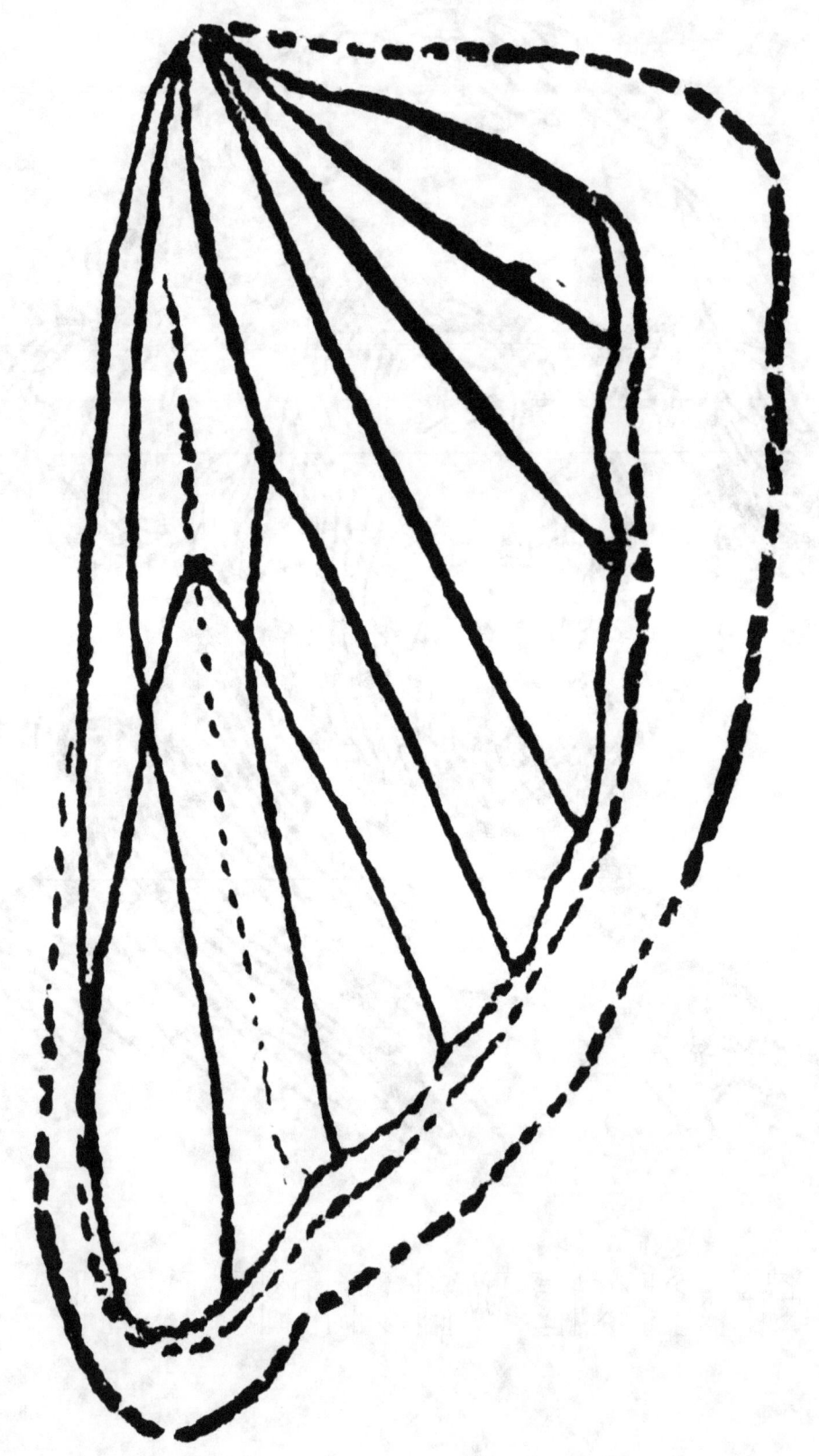

Marjorie's face was as white as a moth's wing.
—Robert Hugh Benson, *Come Rack! Come Rope!* (2001)

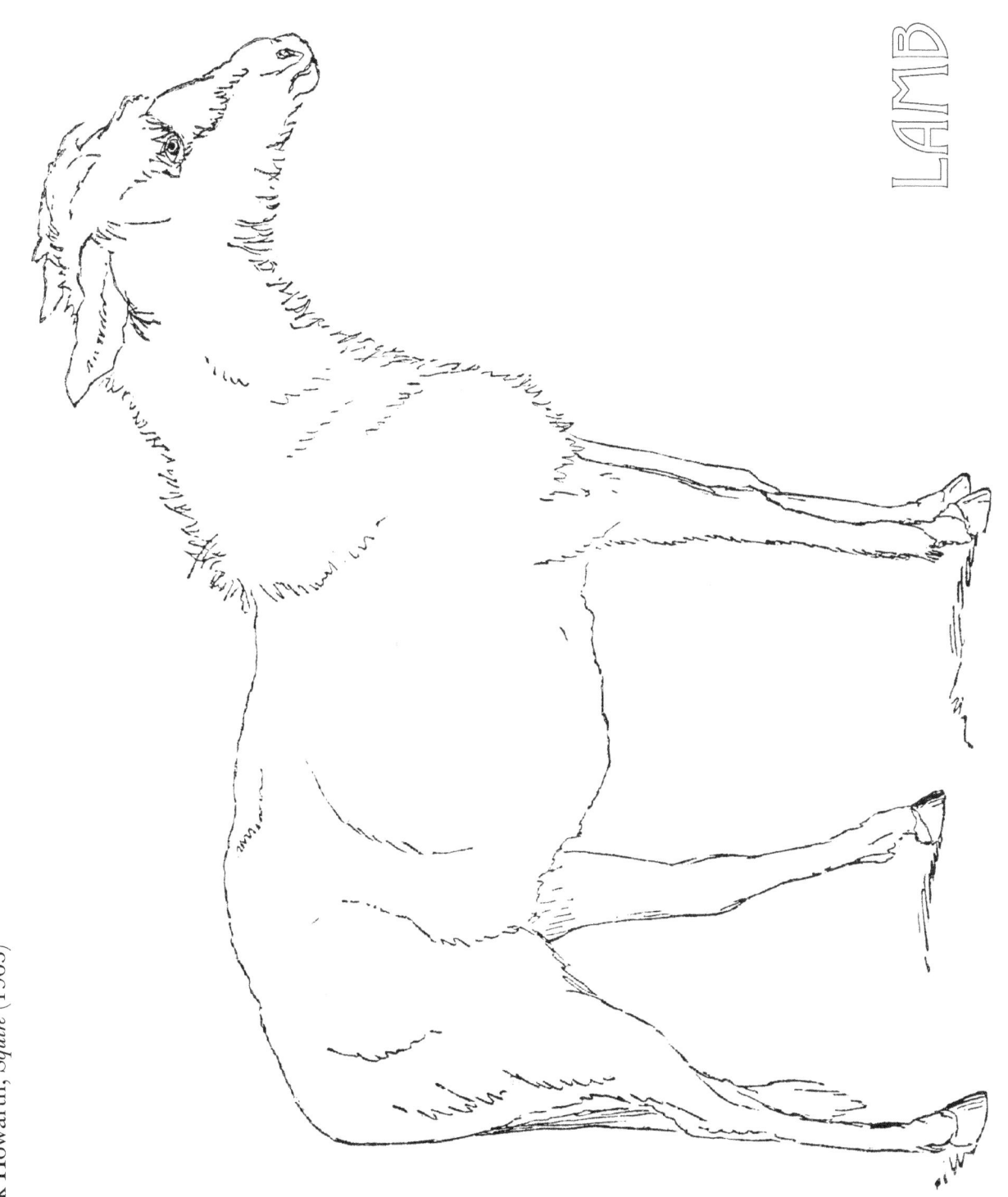

The sheep were as white as clouds that pass.
—Patrick Howarth, *Squire* (1963)

LAMB

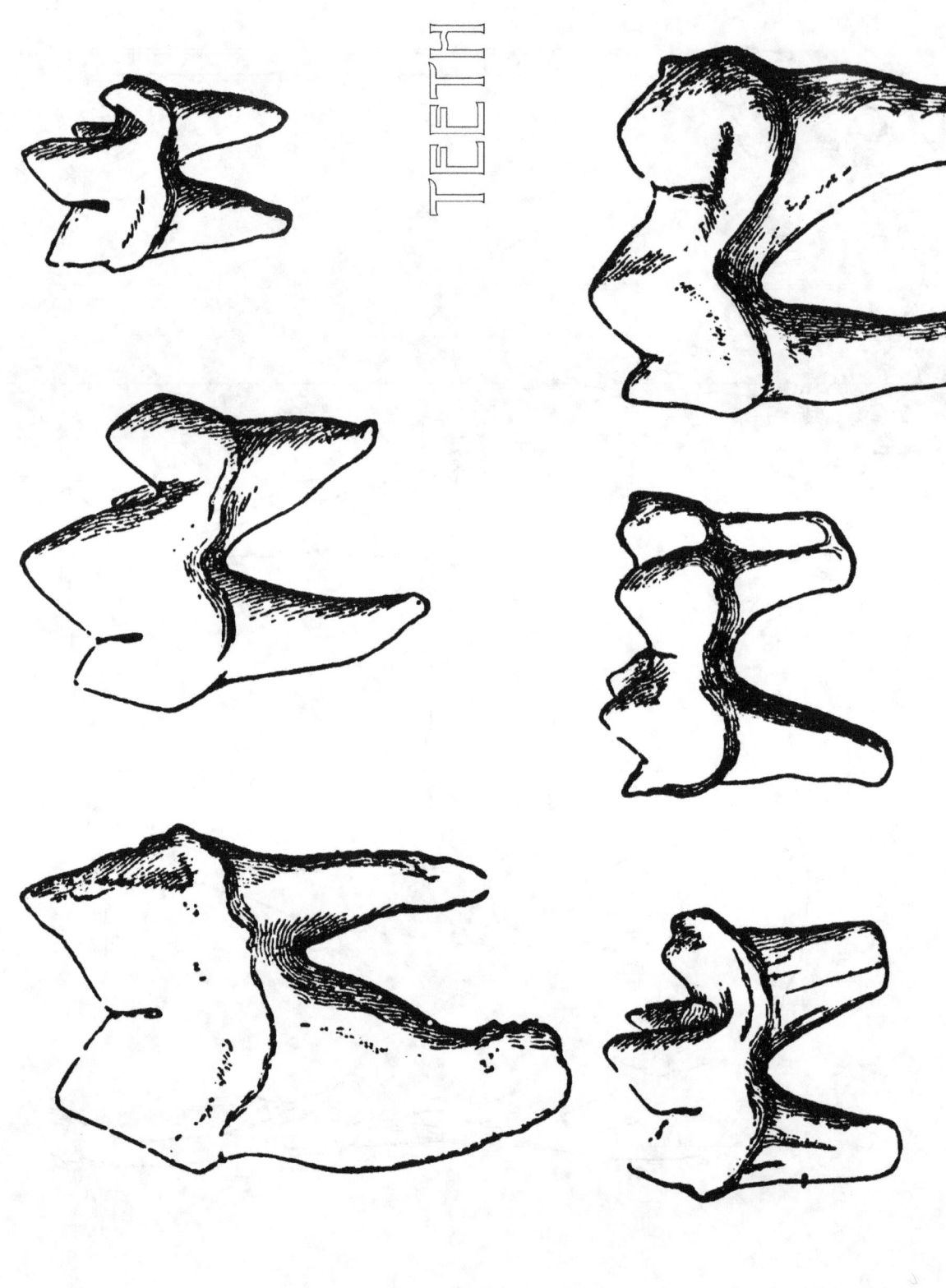

TEETH

She smiled brilliantly, and her white teeth made the world something to chew.
A girl with teeth as white as that need never fear anything.
—Myron Brinig, *Singermann* (1975)

THE WHITE HOUSE

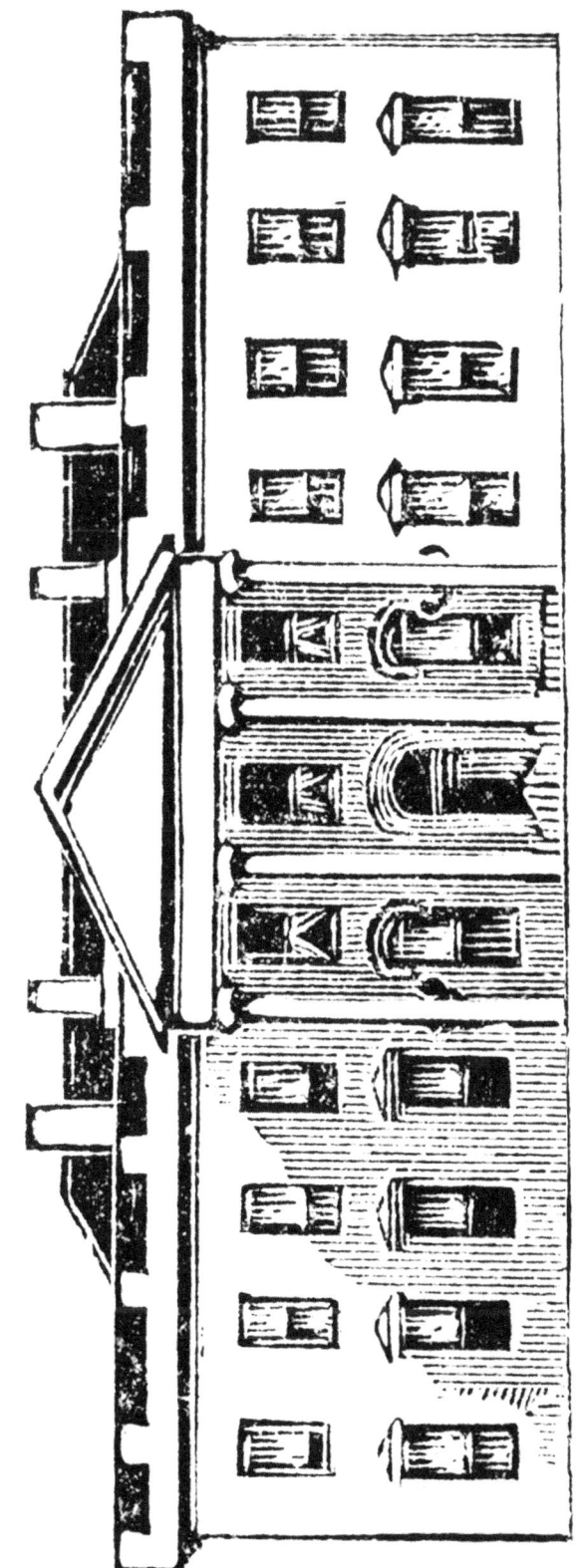

In the vast white house behind him, chamber rising out of chamber, nothing moved.
—John Gardner, *Jason and Medeia* (1973)

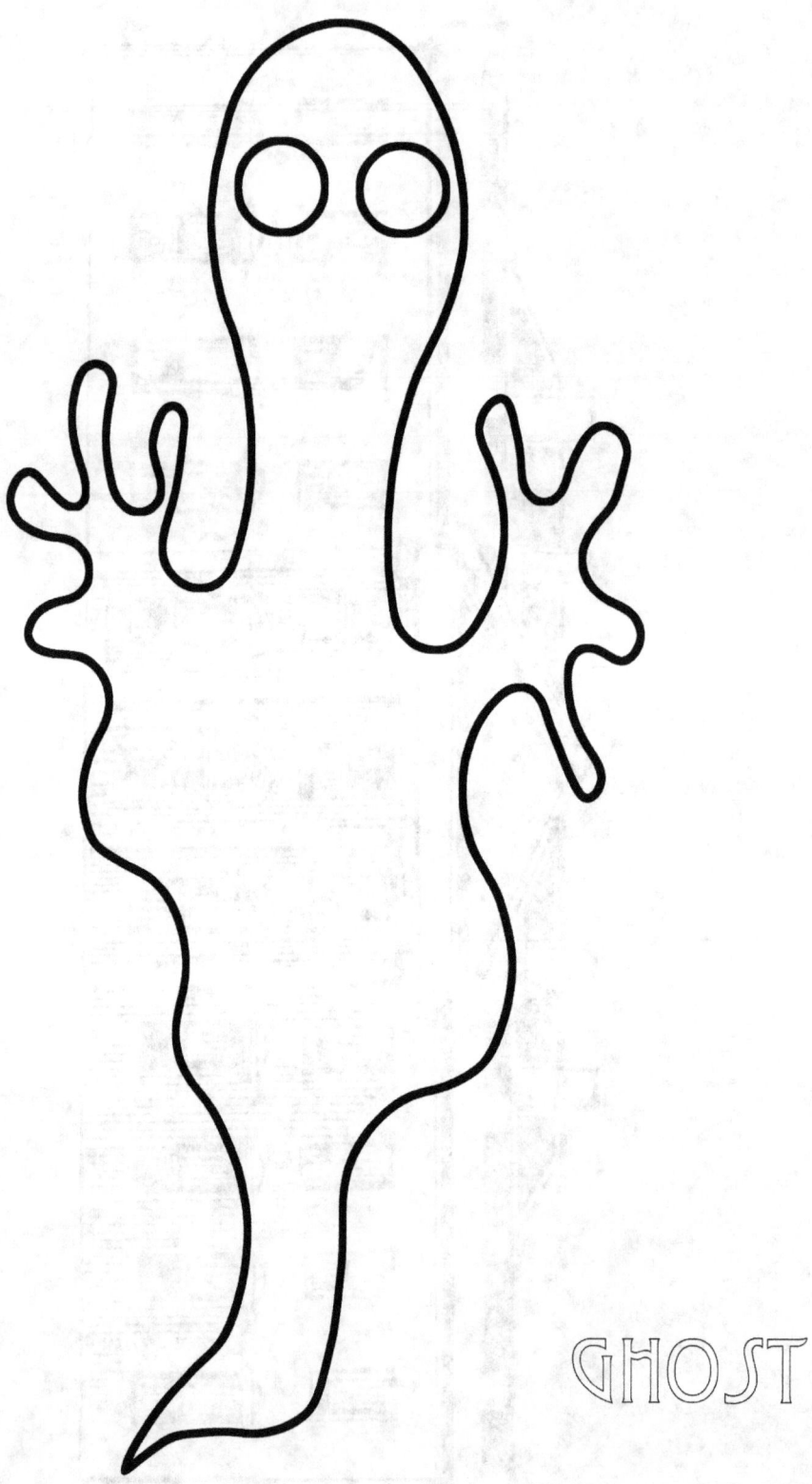

GHOST

Denzil turned as white as a Christmas ghost.
—Israel Zangwill, *The Grey Wig* (1903)

SNOWFLAKE

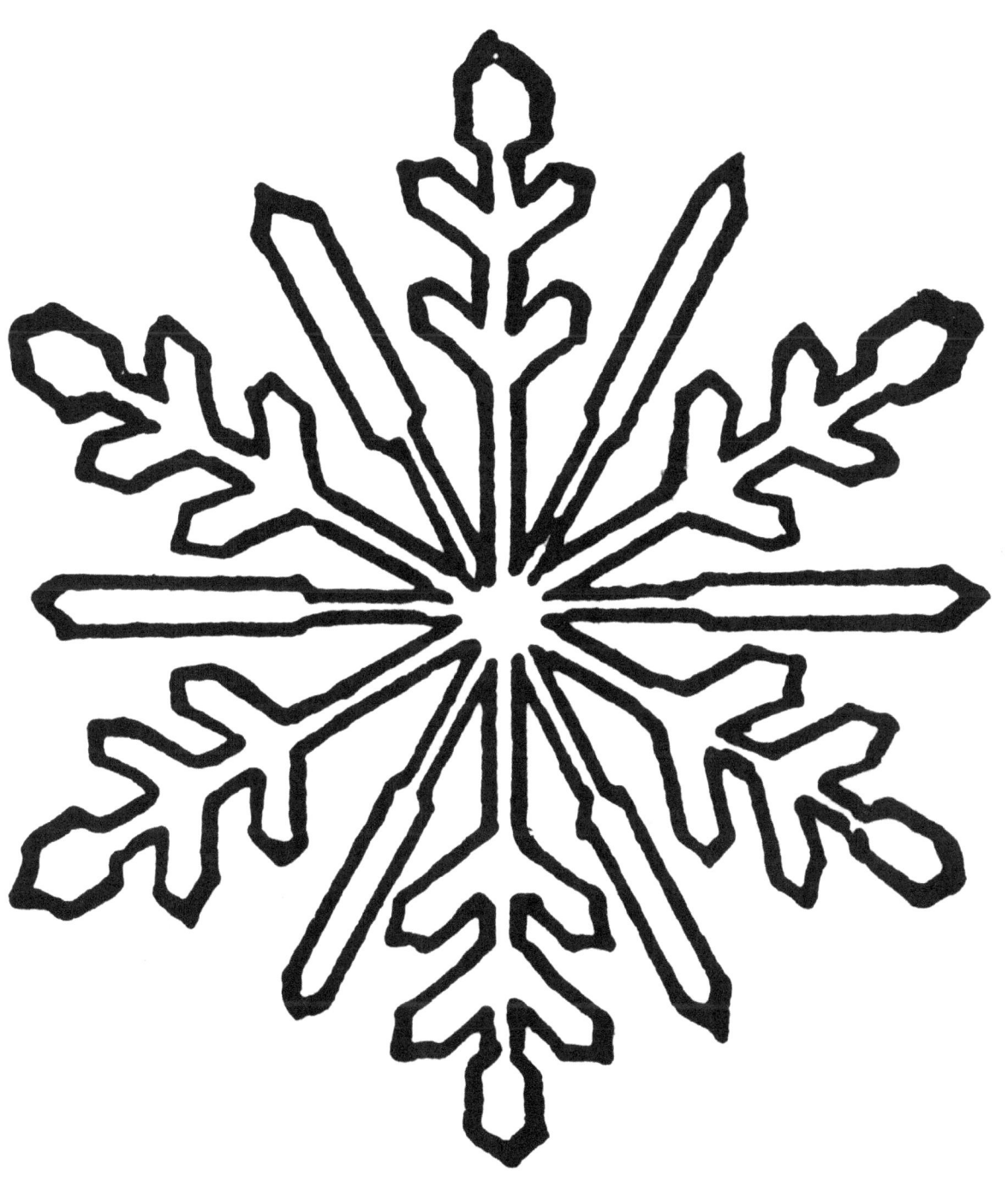

You look like a transfigured snowflake yourself, pet.
—*The New England Magazine* (1917)

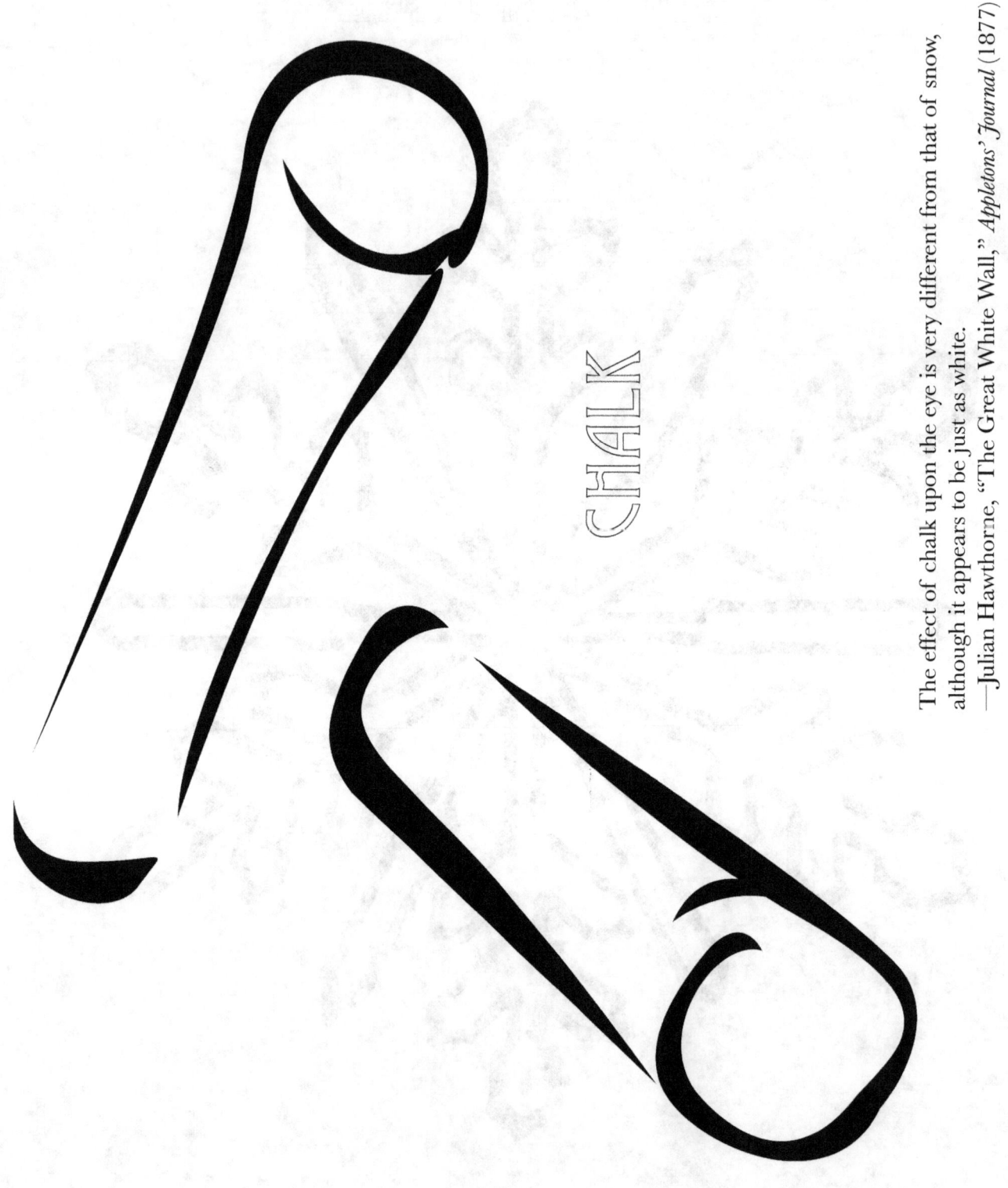

CHALK

The effect of chalk upon the eye is very different from that of snow, although it appears to be just as white.

—Julian Hawthorne, "The Great White Wall," *Appletons' Journal* (1877)

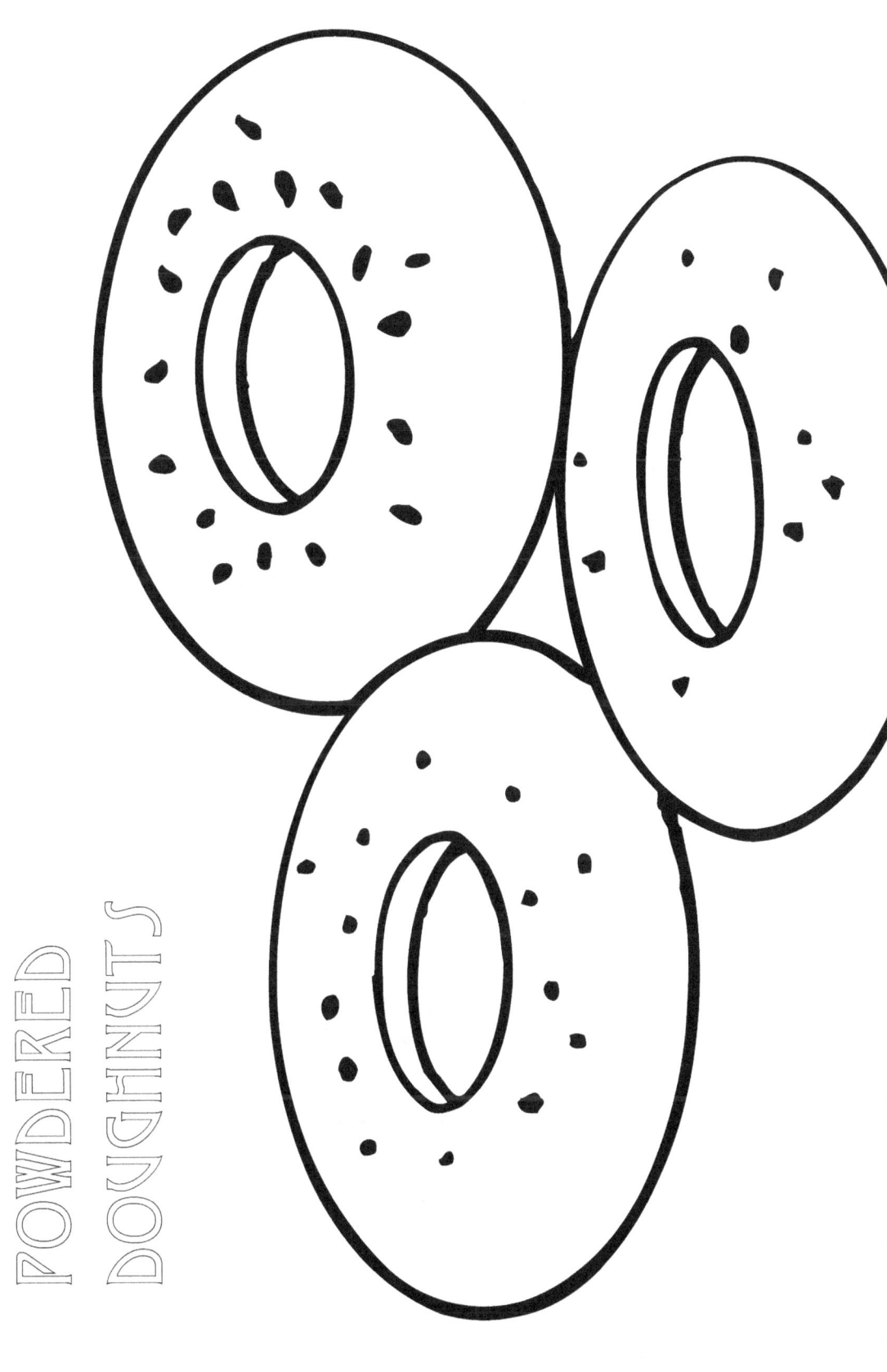

POWDERED
DOUGHNUTS

Sugar walks out of the kitchen eating
a powdered donut, his mouth ringed white.
—Brad Barkley, *Another Perfect Catastrophe* (2004)

BLANK BOOK ON PILLOW

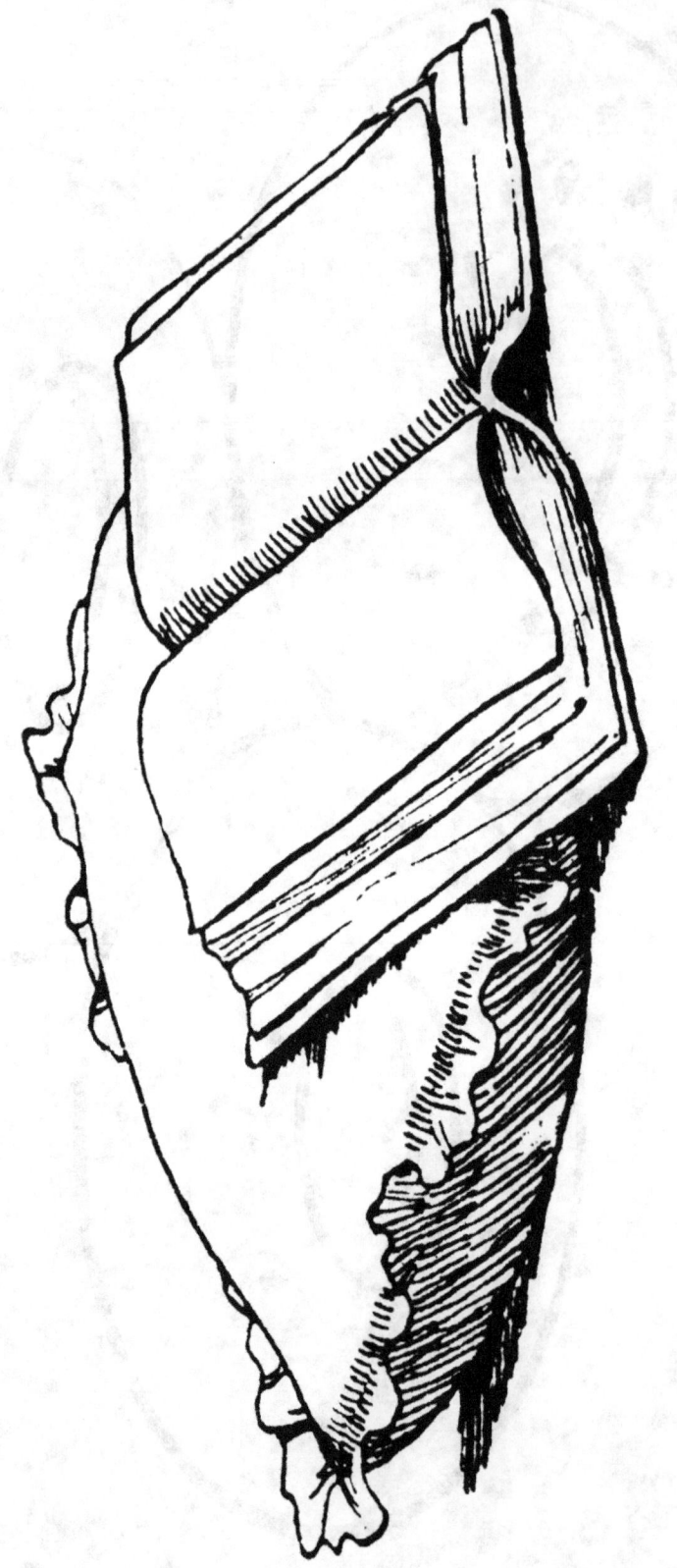

It was propped against her pillow, as white and smooth as the clean sheets.
—Catherine Chidgey, *The Strength of the Sun* (2002)

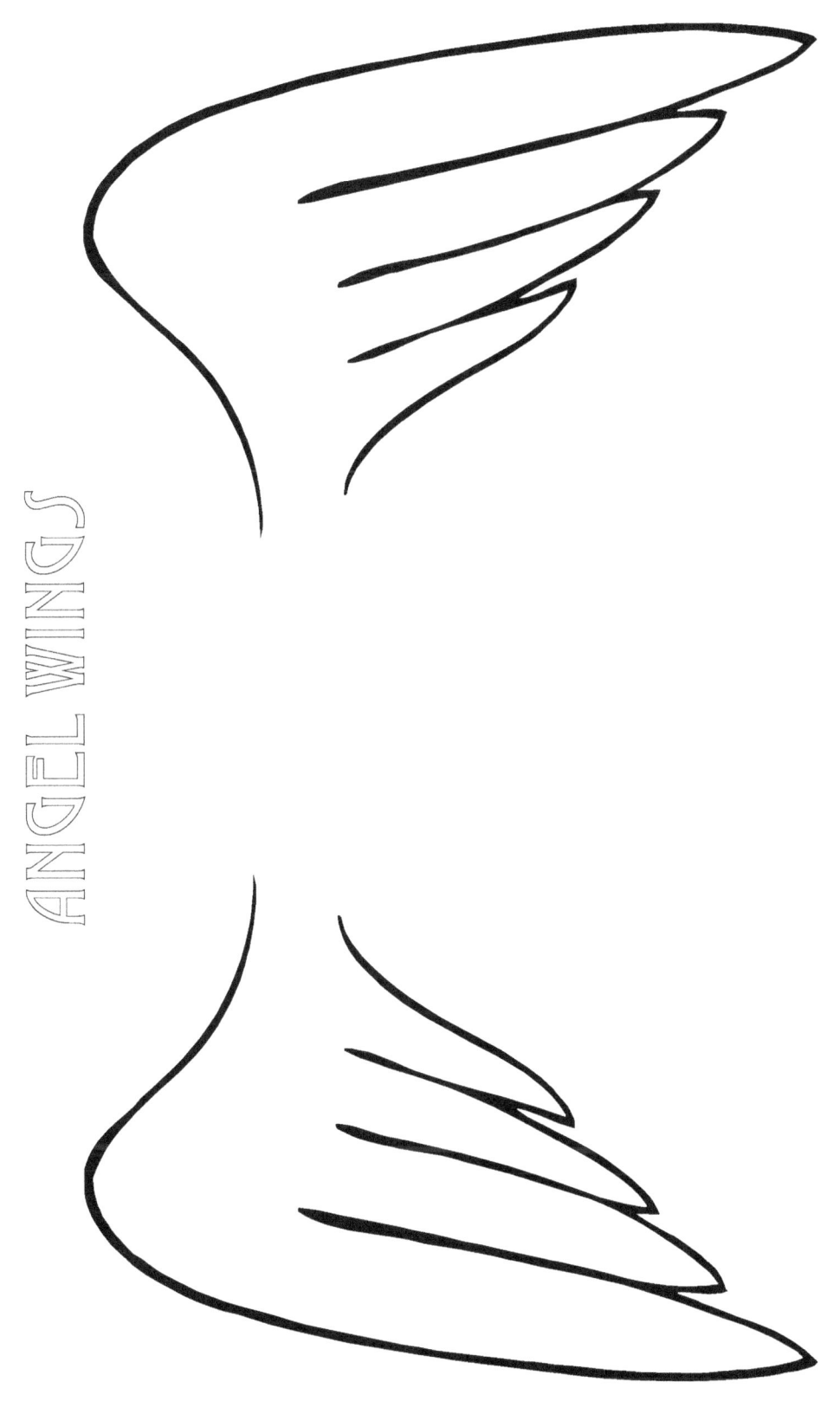

ANGEL WINGS

One has heard poets speak of a quill dropped from an angel's wing. That is the kind of nib of which I feel in need to-night. . . . Whitest paper, newest pen, ear sensitive, tremulous; heart pure and mind open, broad and clear as the blue air for the most delicate gossamer thoughts to wing through; and snow-white words, lily-white words, words of ivory and pearl, words of silver and alabaster, words white as hawthorn and daisy, words white as morning milk, words 'whiter than Venus' doves, and softer than the down beneath their wings—virginal, saintlike, nunnery words.

—Richard Le Gallienne, *Prose Fancies* (1894)

MVSHROOMS

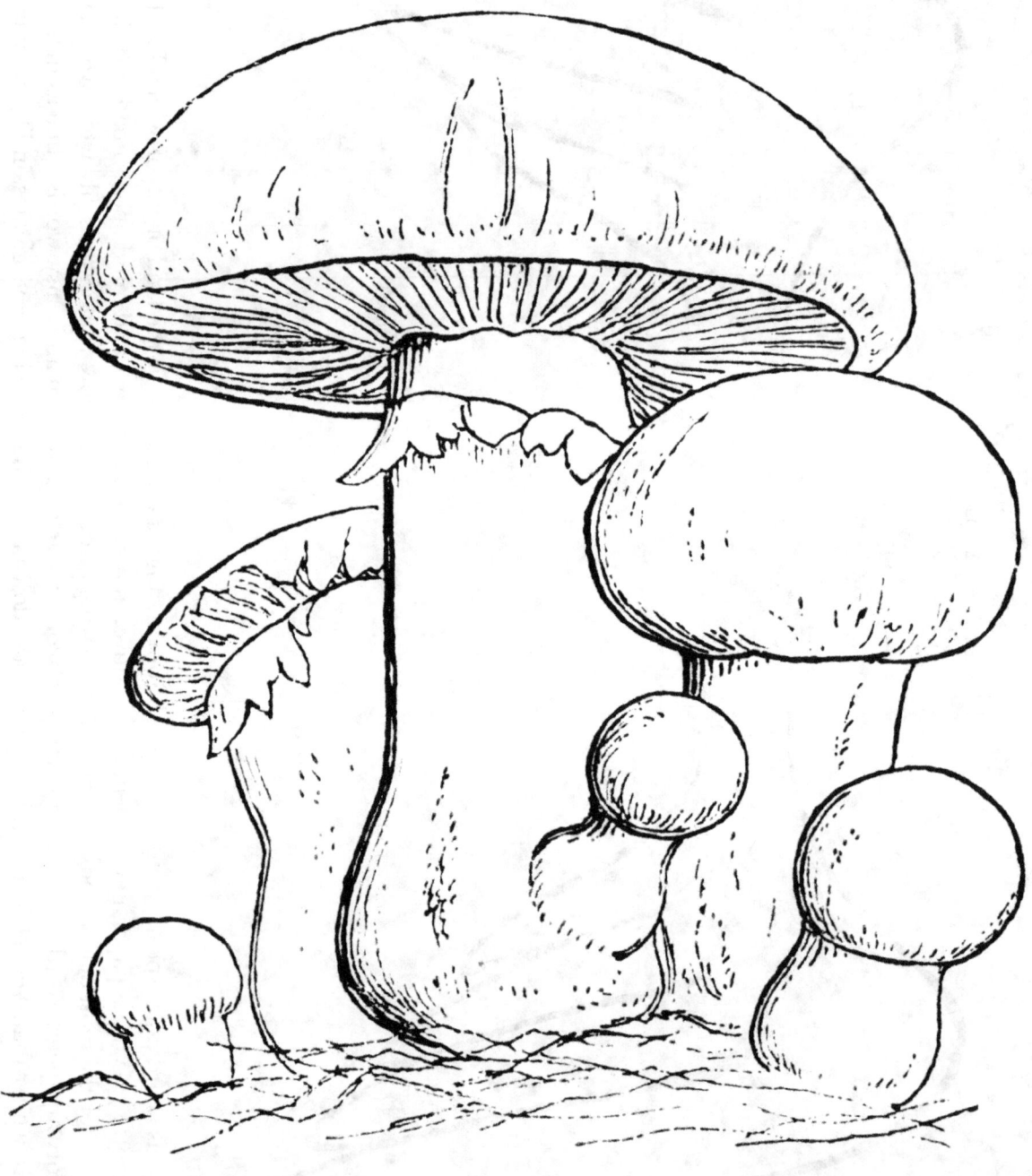

An old arthritic nun with a mushroom complexion under her white coif came
and laid a hand as white and speckled as another mushroom on my mother's.
—Aidan Higgins, *Balcony of Europe* (1972)

PARAFFIN CANDLE

As a white candle
In a holy place,
So is the beauty
Of an agéd face.
—Joseph Campbell,
"The Old Woman" (c. 1940)

IVORY TUSKS

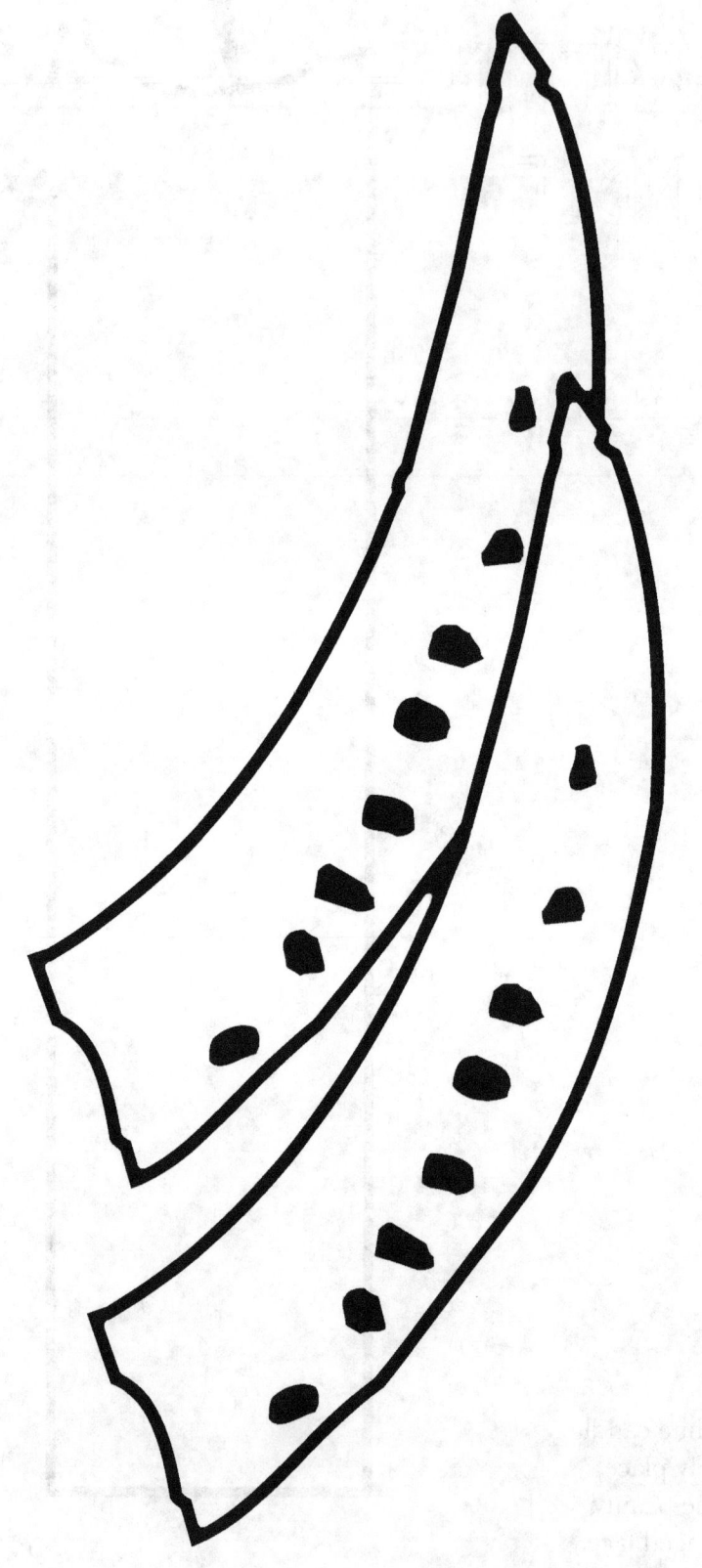

Beautiful Adonis lies in the mountains, his thigh by a white tusk gored, white thigh by white tusk.
—Bion, "Lament for Adonis" (late 2nd century BC), *Anthology of Classical Myth*, edited and translated by Stephen Trzaskoma, Thomas G. Palaima, R. Scott Smith

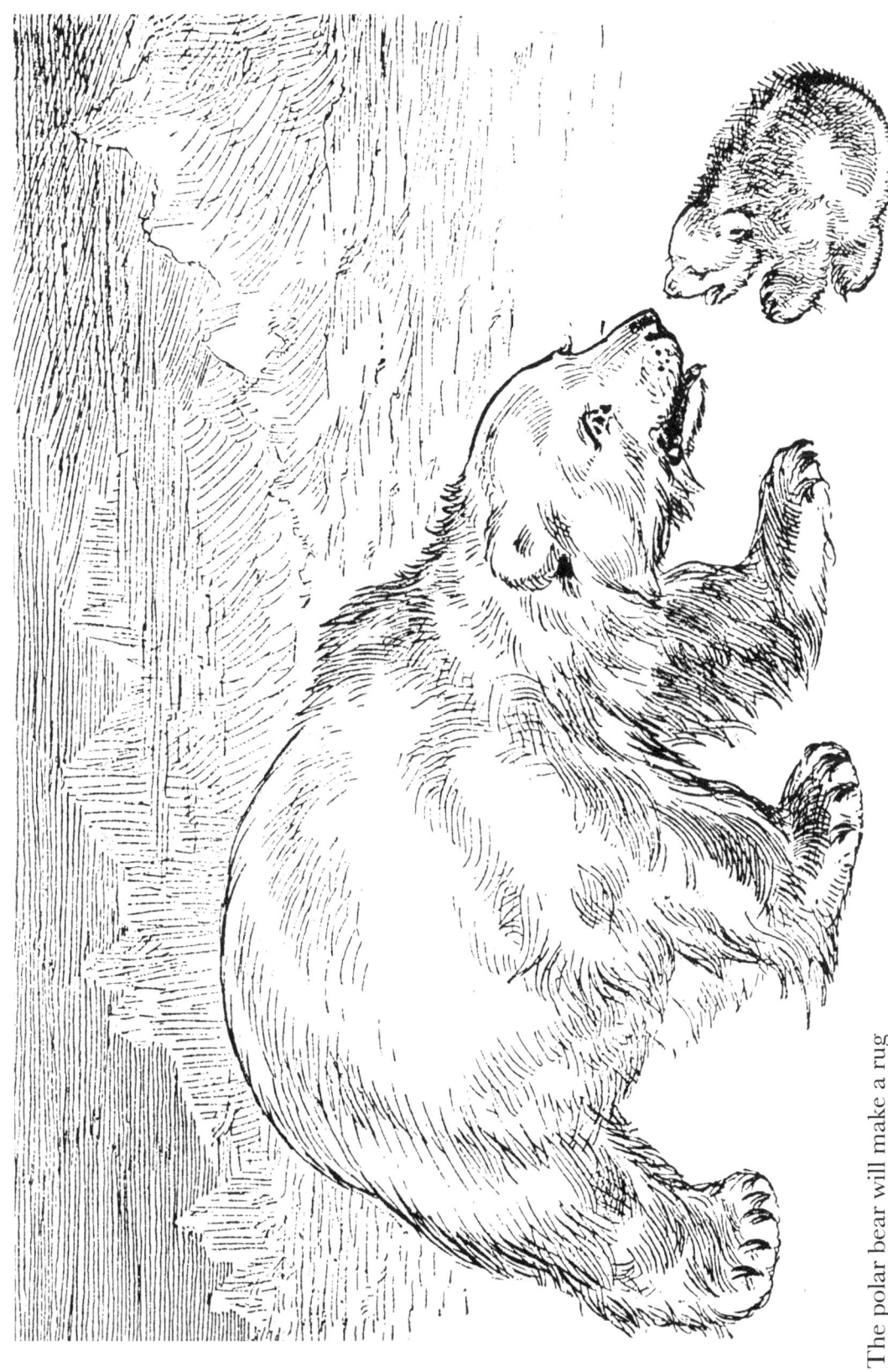

POLAR BEARS

The polar bear will make a rug
Almost as white as snow:
But if he gets you in his hug,
He rarely lets you go.

—E. V. Lucas, *A Book of Verses*
for Children (1970)

JASMINE BLOSSOM

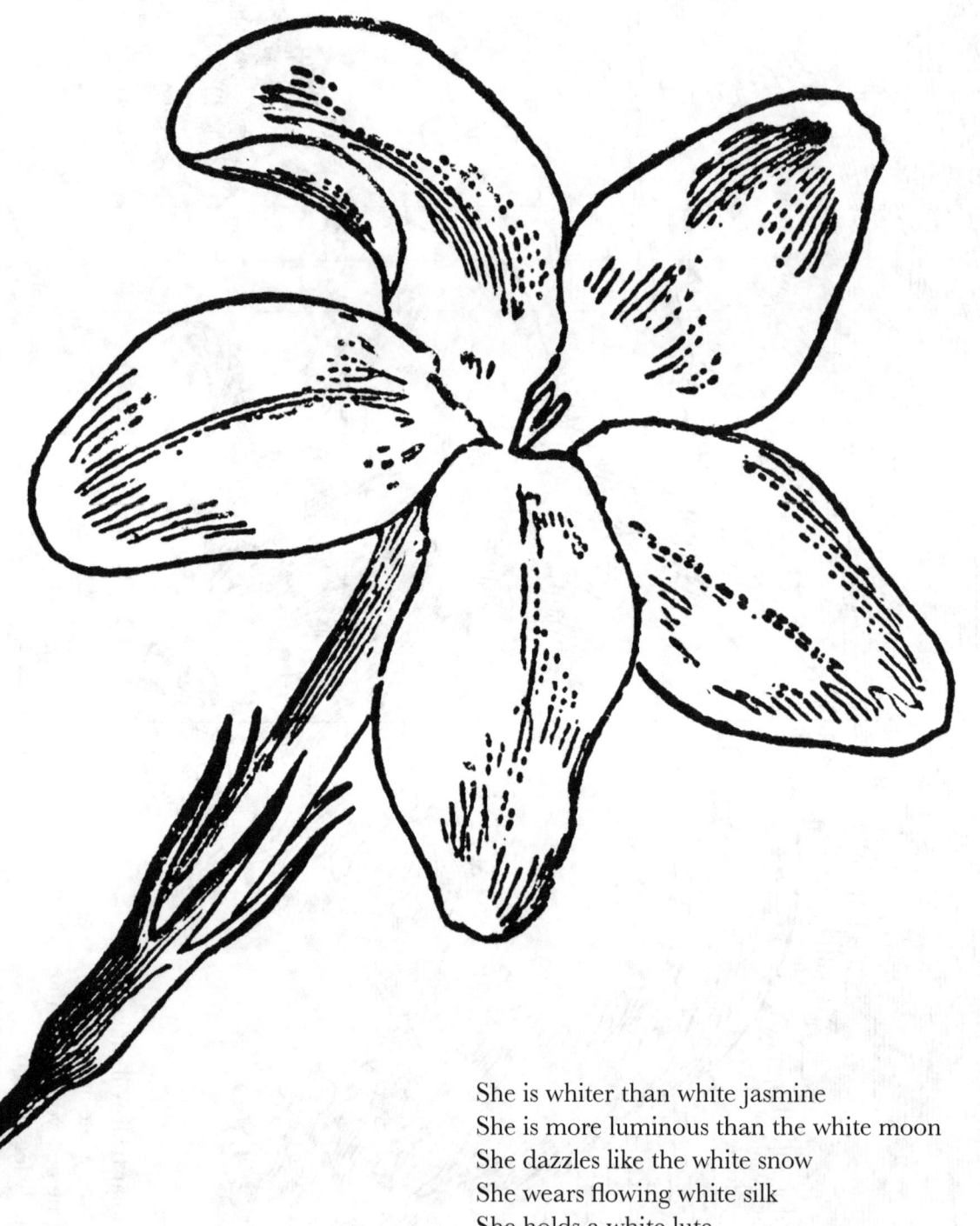

She is whiter than white jasmine
She is more luminous than the white moon
She dazzles like the white snow
She wears flowing white silk
She holds a white lute
She is seated on a white lotus
—"Saraswati As She Appears As White Radiance
of Knowledge" (translated by Gita Das, 1996)

PEARL NECKLACE

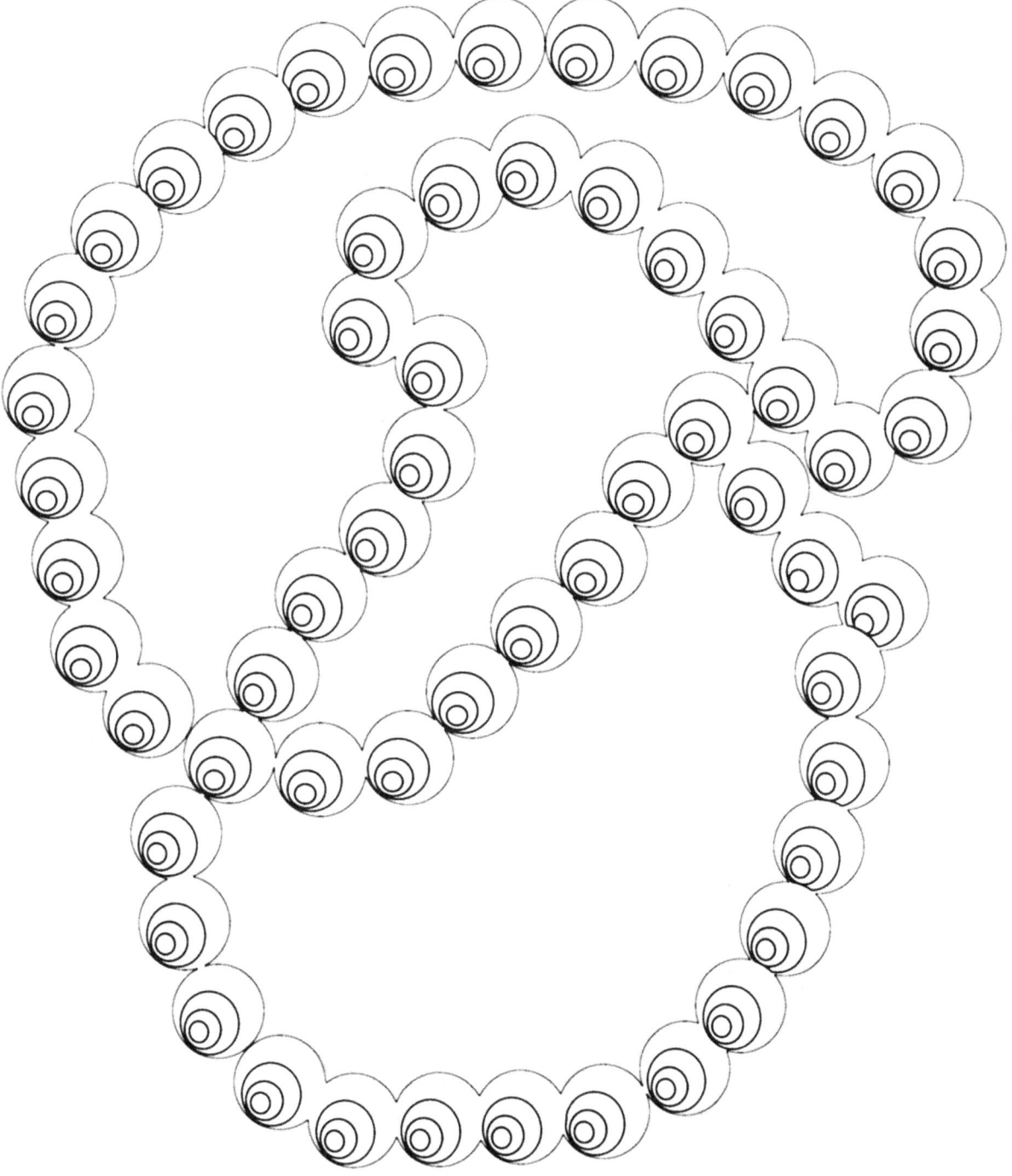

Pearls as white as cottage cheese, every one of which is worth an eye.
—Miguel de Cervantes, *Don Quixote* (1605)

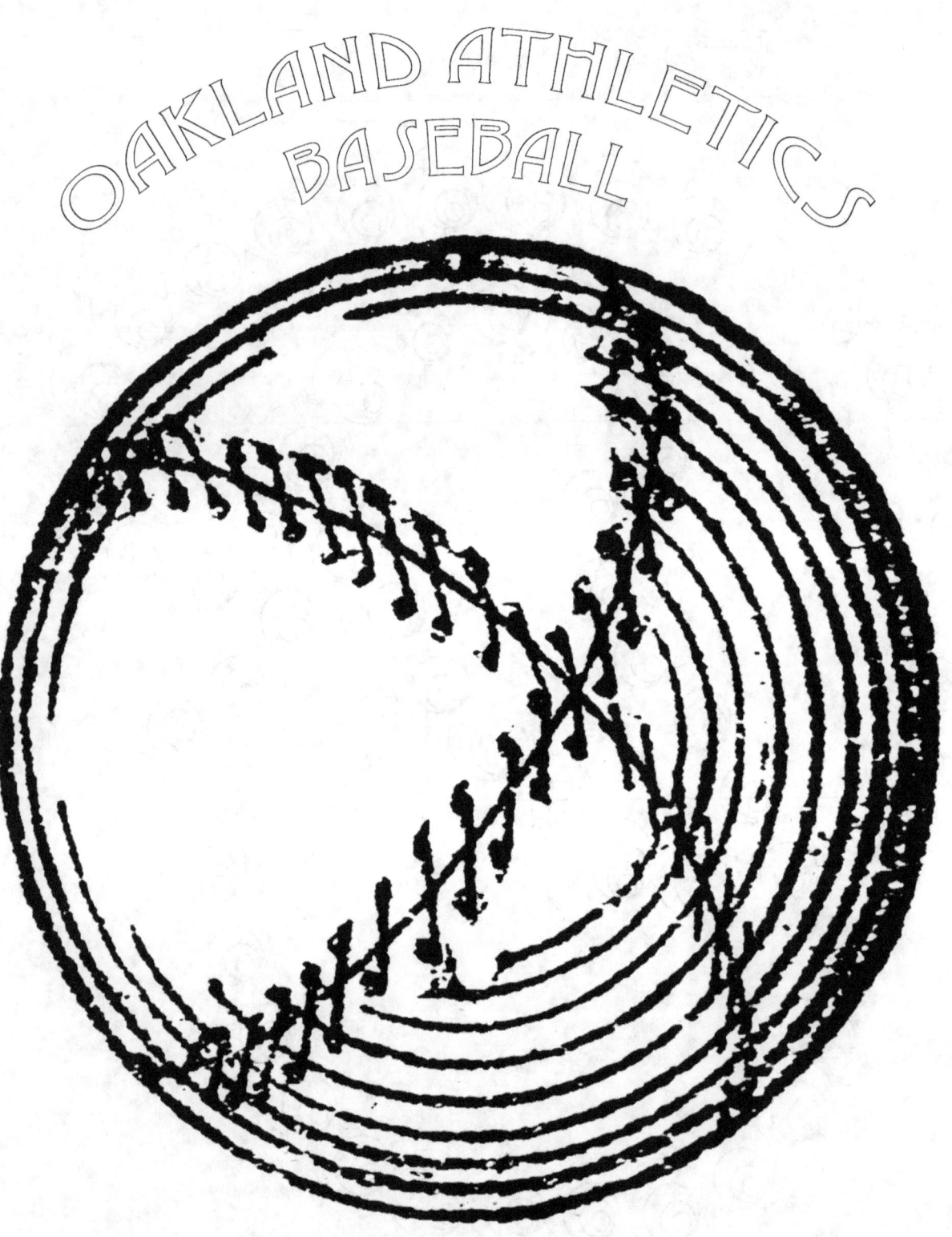

OAKLAND ATHLETICS
BASEBALL

White baseball against white cotton.
—Roger Kahn, *Into My Own* (2006)

LINEN DRESS

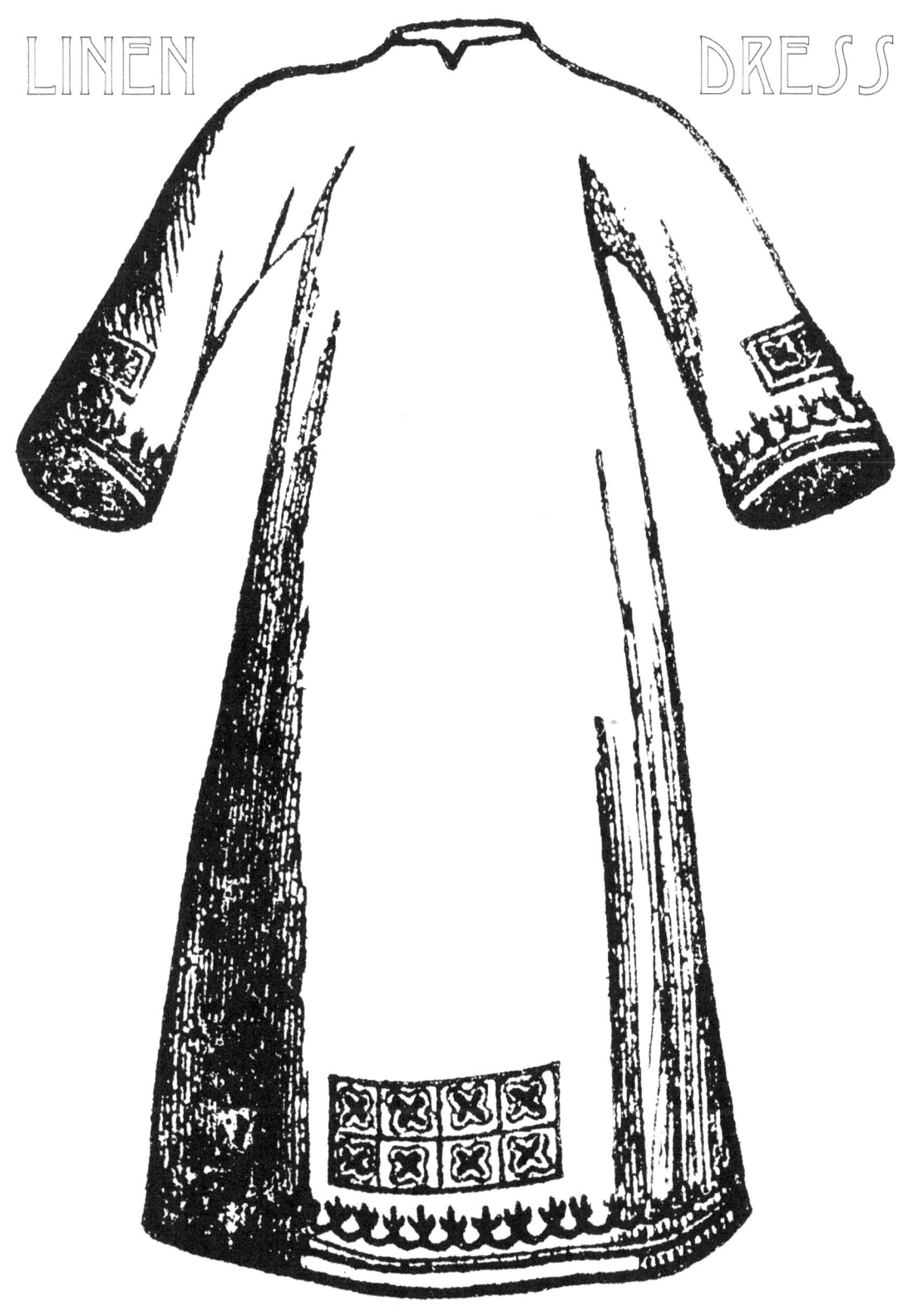

Linen, so clean and white as to be a fit emblem of the righteousness of saints.
—Alex Johnston Warden, *The Linen Trade, Ancient and Modern* (1867)

ICE CREAM

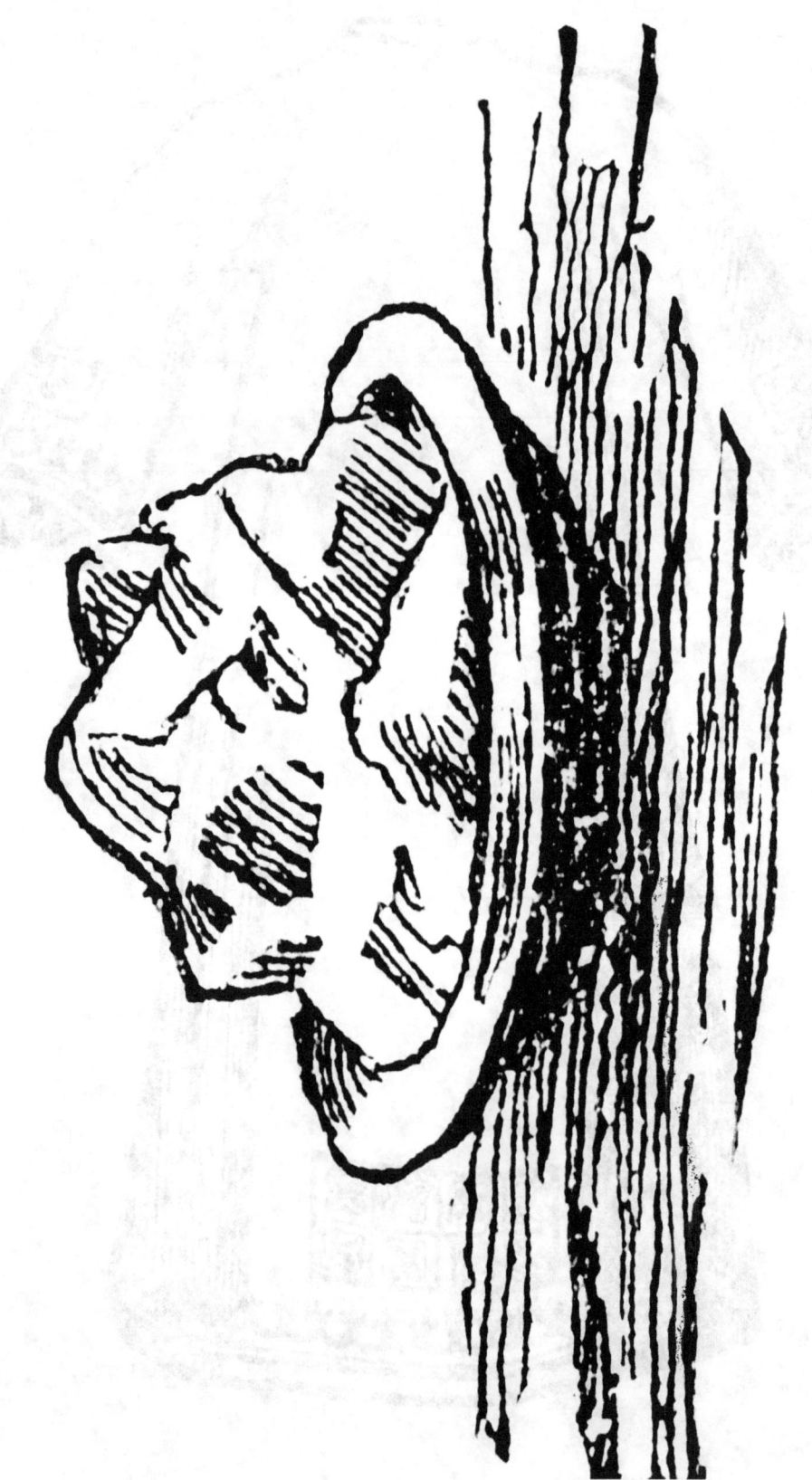

No, not pale, white. As white as vanilla ice-cream.
—John Marsden, *The Other Side of Dawn* (2002)

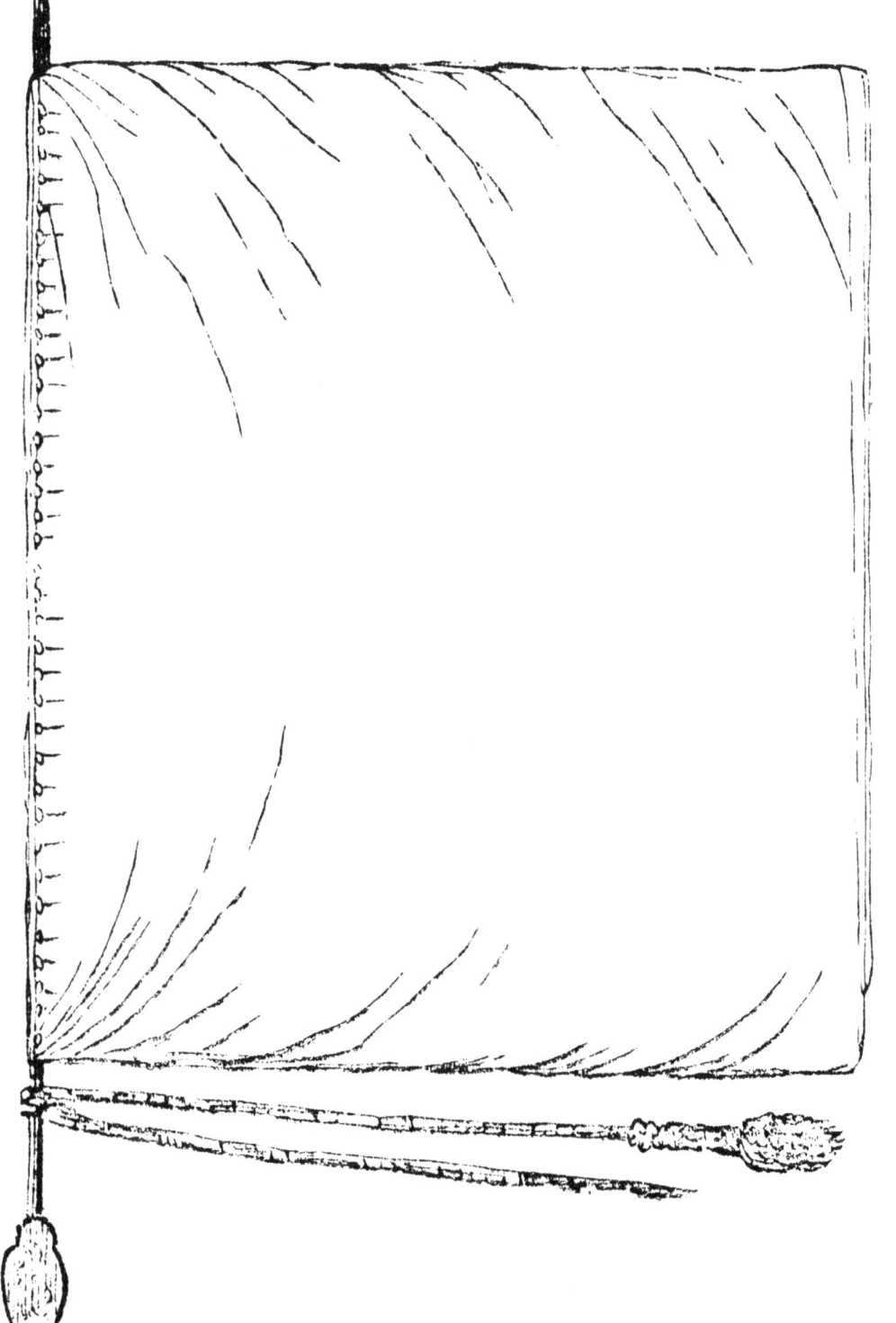

FLAG OF TRUCE

A few more years and there will be nothing but the white of our empty chairs around a table, white as the white flag of our shared surrender.

—Marie Claire Blais, *These Festive Nights* (translated by Sheila Fischman, 1997)

TURTLE'S UNDERBELLY

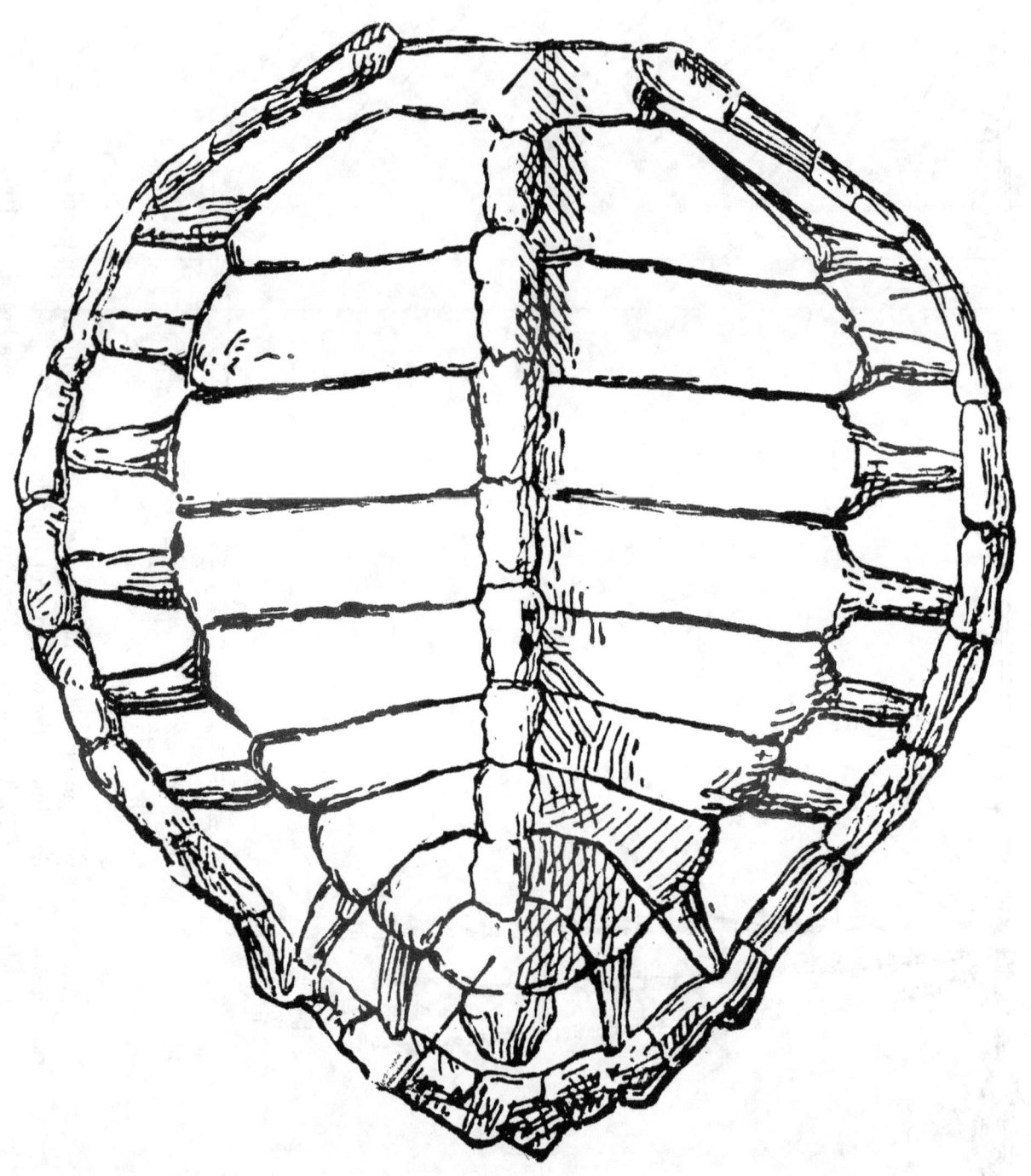

To all appearances, the white turtle lay quietly on the rock unmoving, as if it were practicing meditation.
—Chen Kaiguo and Zheng Shunchao, *Opening the Dragon Gate* (translated by Thomas F. Cleary, 1996)

SNOWSHOE HARE

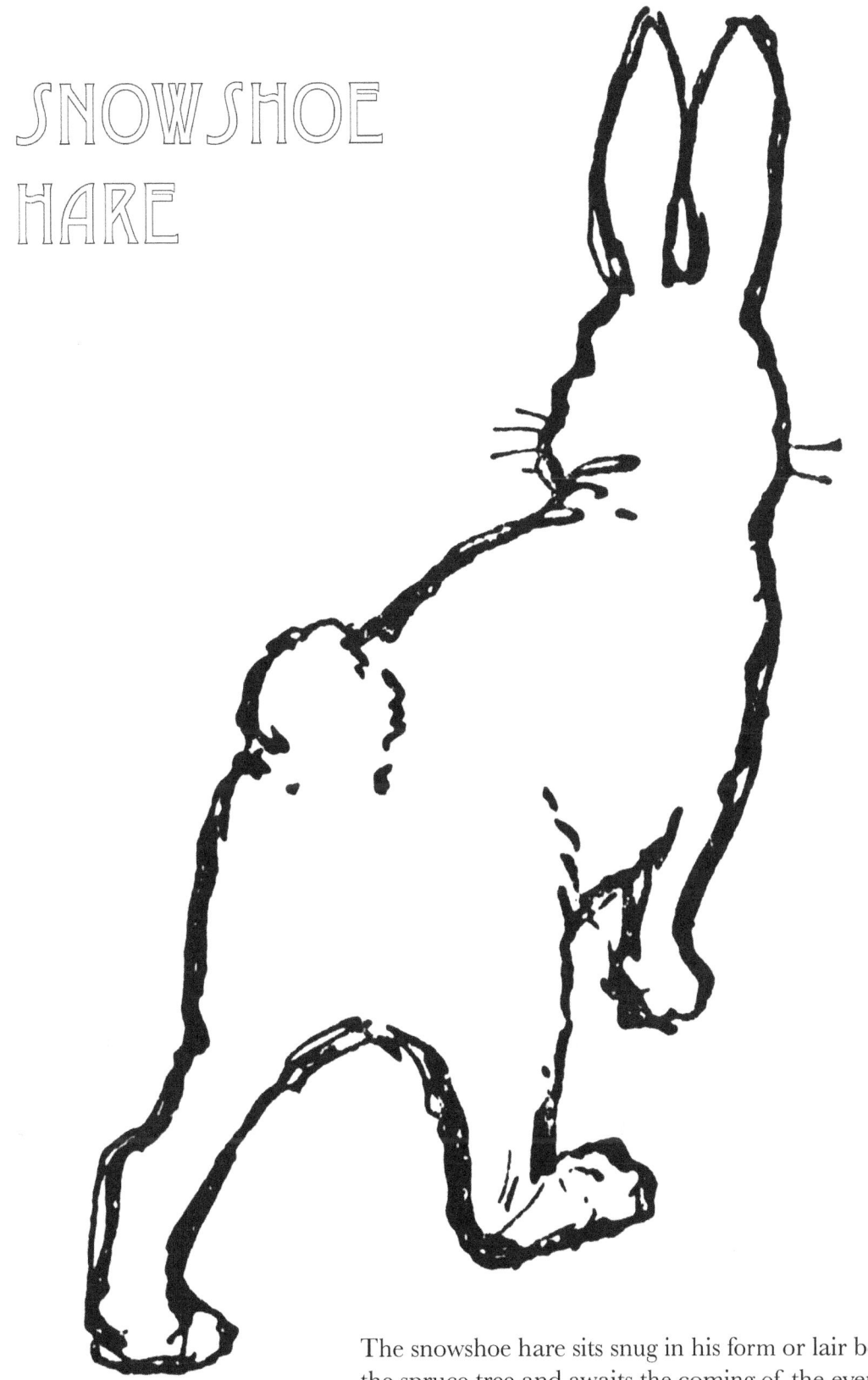

The snowshoe hare sits snug in his form or lair beneath the spruce tree and awaits the coming of the evening's darkness under whose cover he will venture forth to feed.
—Hudson's Bay Company, *The Beaver* (1920)

PELICAN

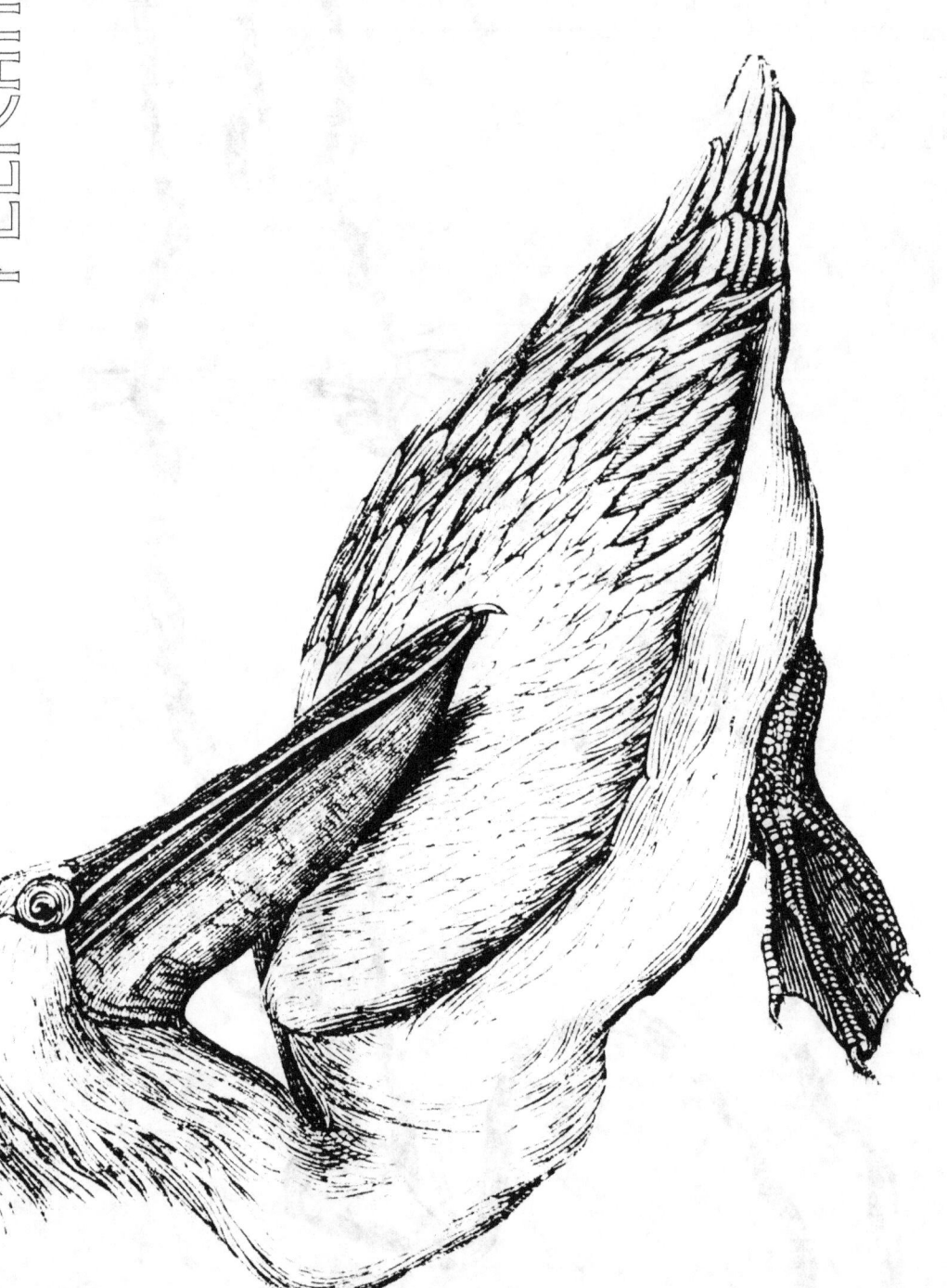

You are looking for bald eagles perching in nearby trees when you spot a white pelican, silently and gracefully passing just overhead.
—Kevin M. Lohraff, *Hiking Missouri* (1999)

WHITE BLOOD CELLS

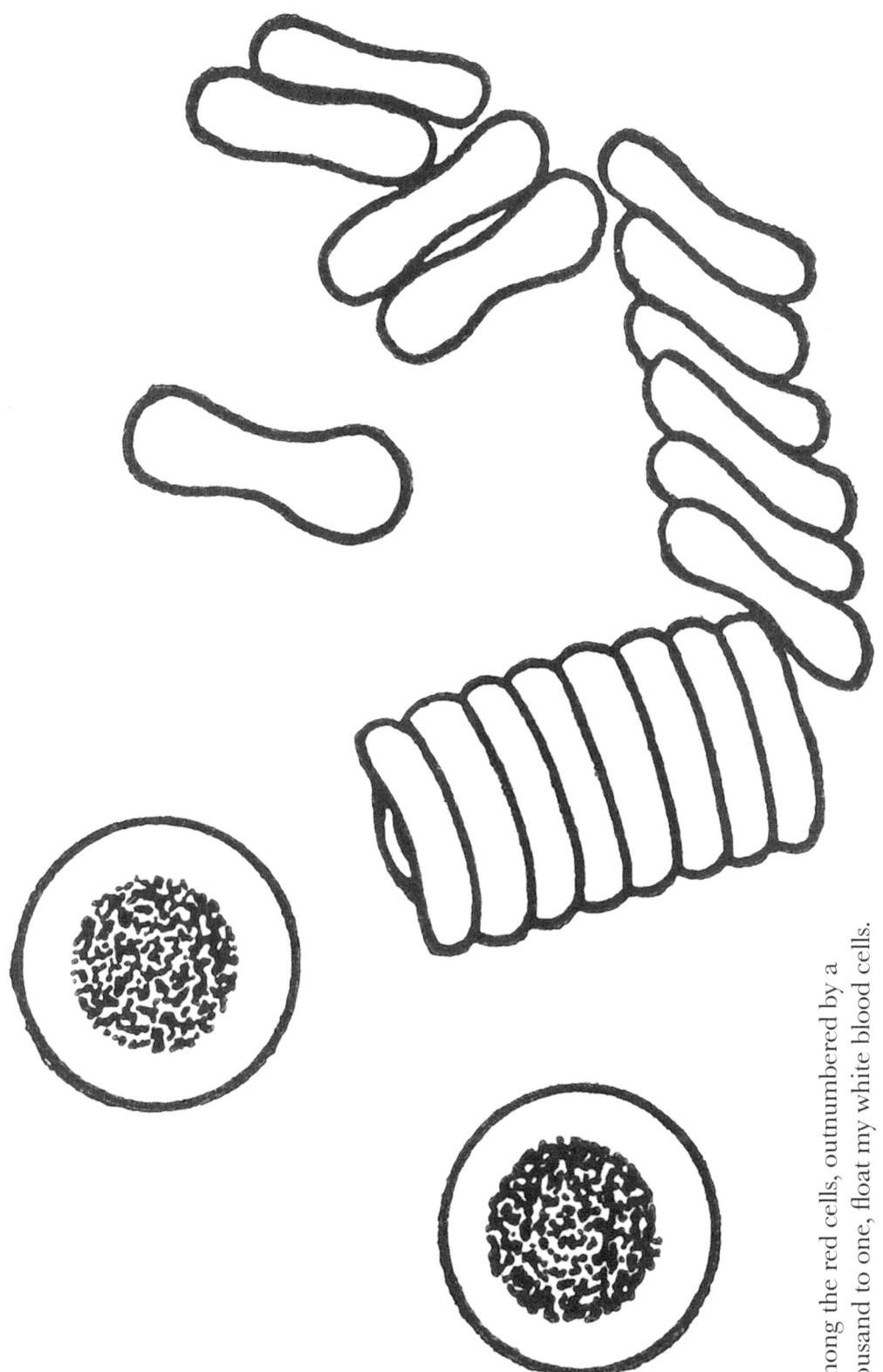

Among the red cells, outnumbered by a thousand to one, float my white blood cells.
—Bryan Sykes, *Adam's Curse* (2004)

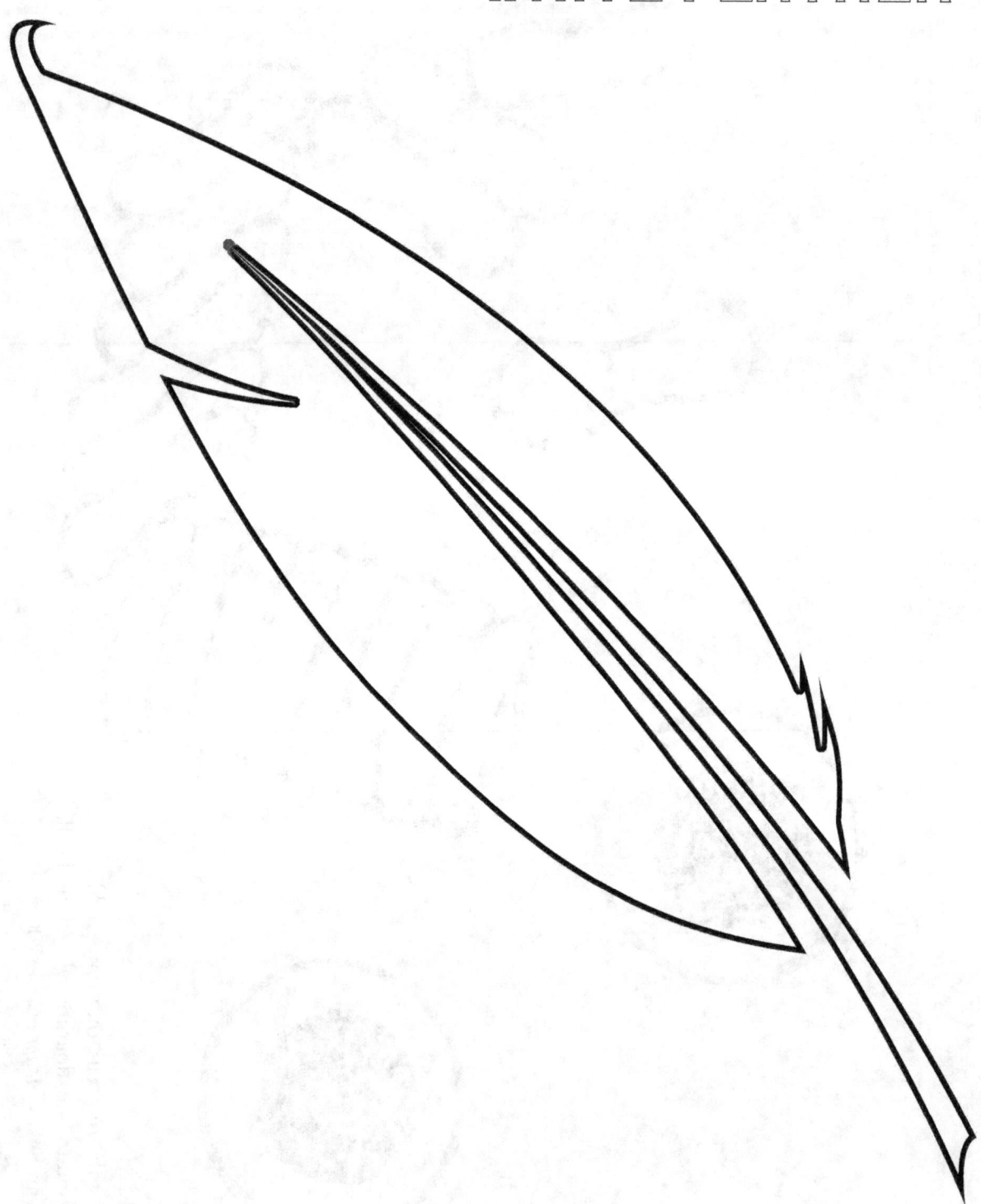

The white feather sent a long beam of white light to the east.
—Morris Edward Opler, *Myths and Tales of the Jicarilla Apache Indians* (1974)

2%

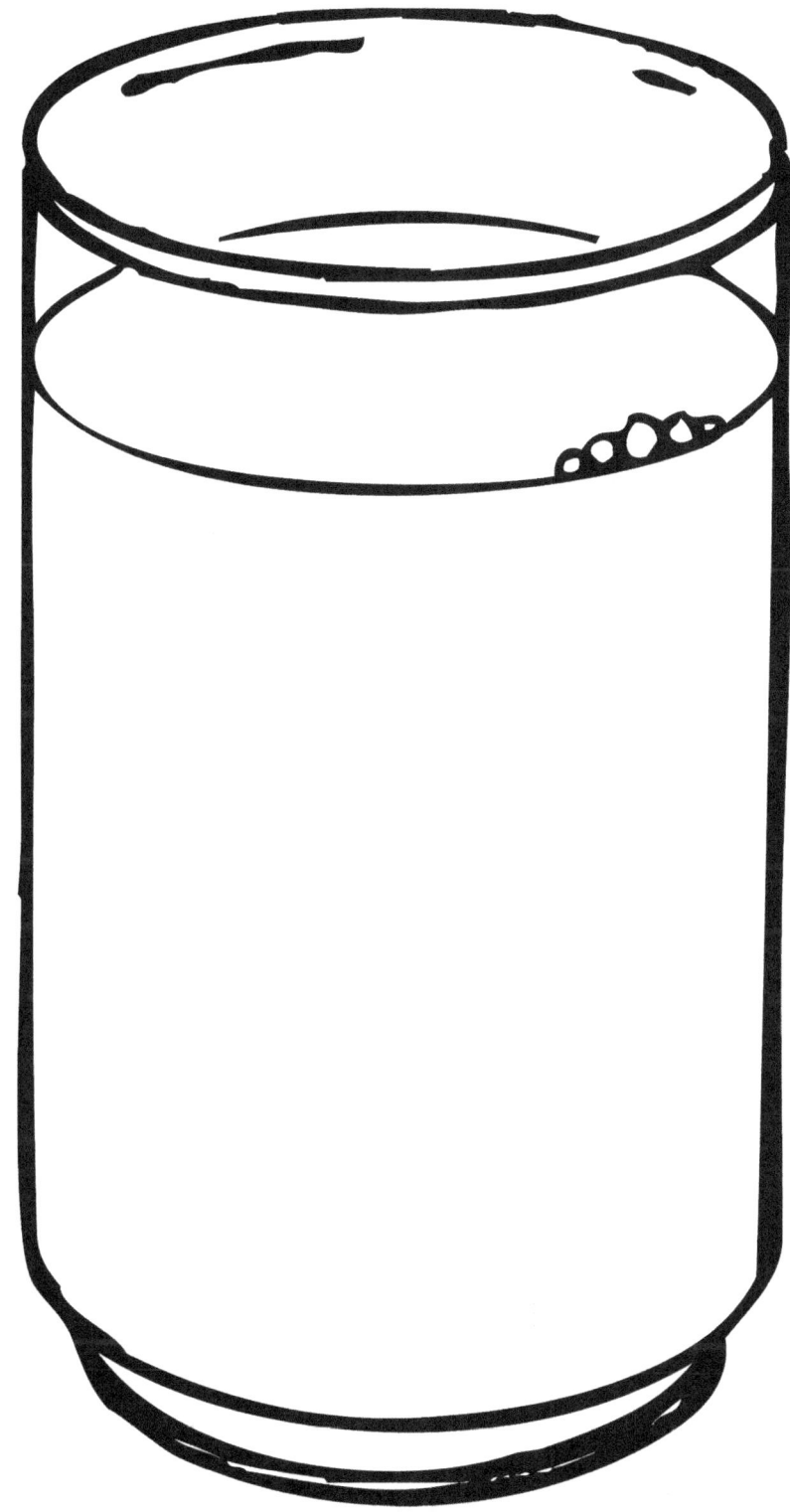

His image of her fades to a screen of purest white as he gazes at the white glass of milk on the white tablecloth, the white crysanthemums, the white tile oven and the white faces.
—Linda Haverty Rugg, *Picturing Ourselves* (1997)

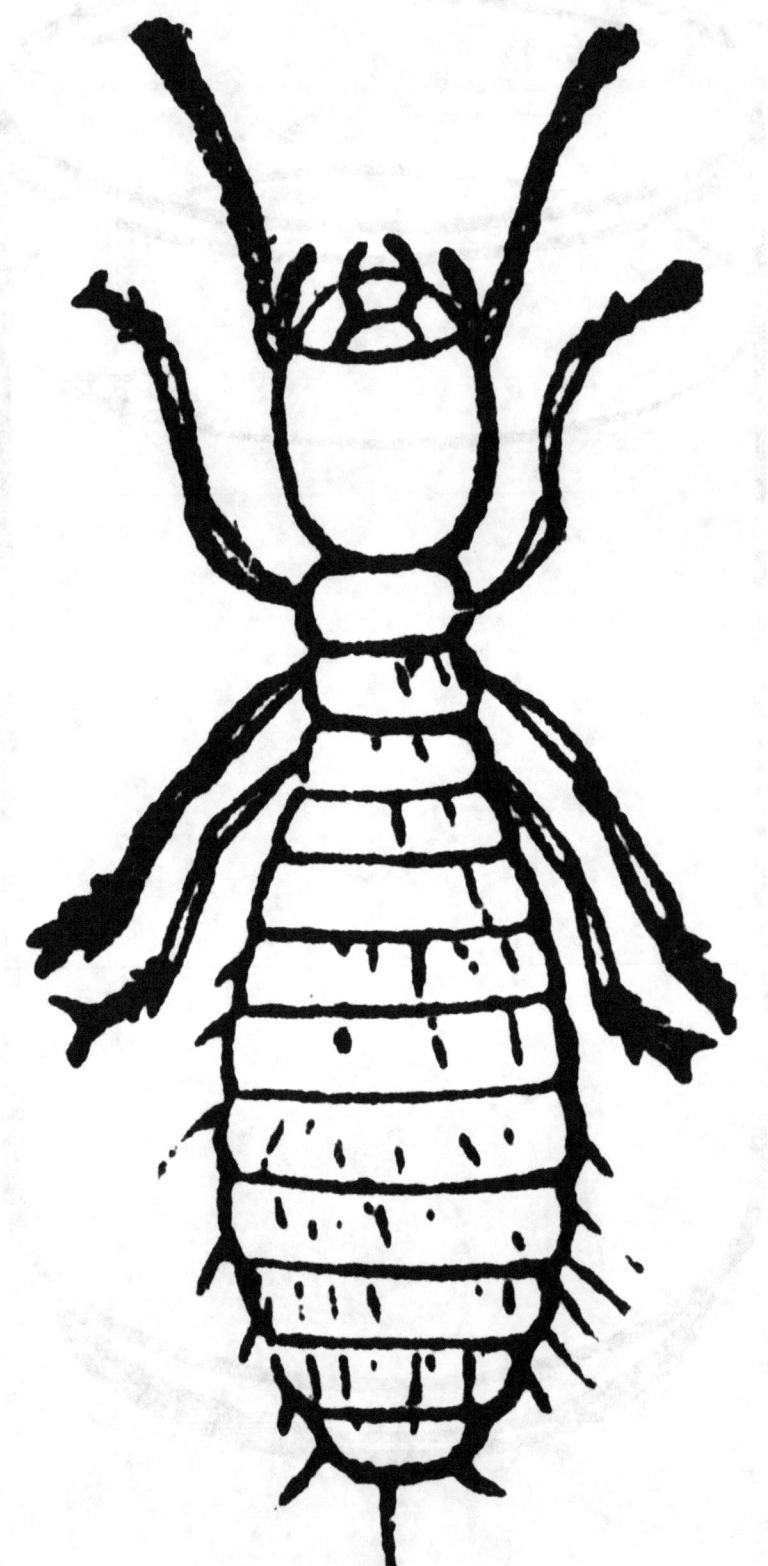

Elderly clerks white as termites move sluggishly along the corridors, as if beginning to stir after a long hibernation.
—John Dos Passos, *In All Countries* (1934)

TERMITE

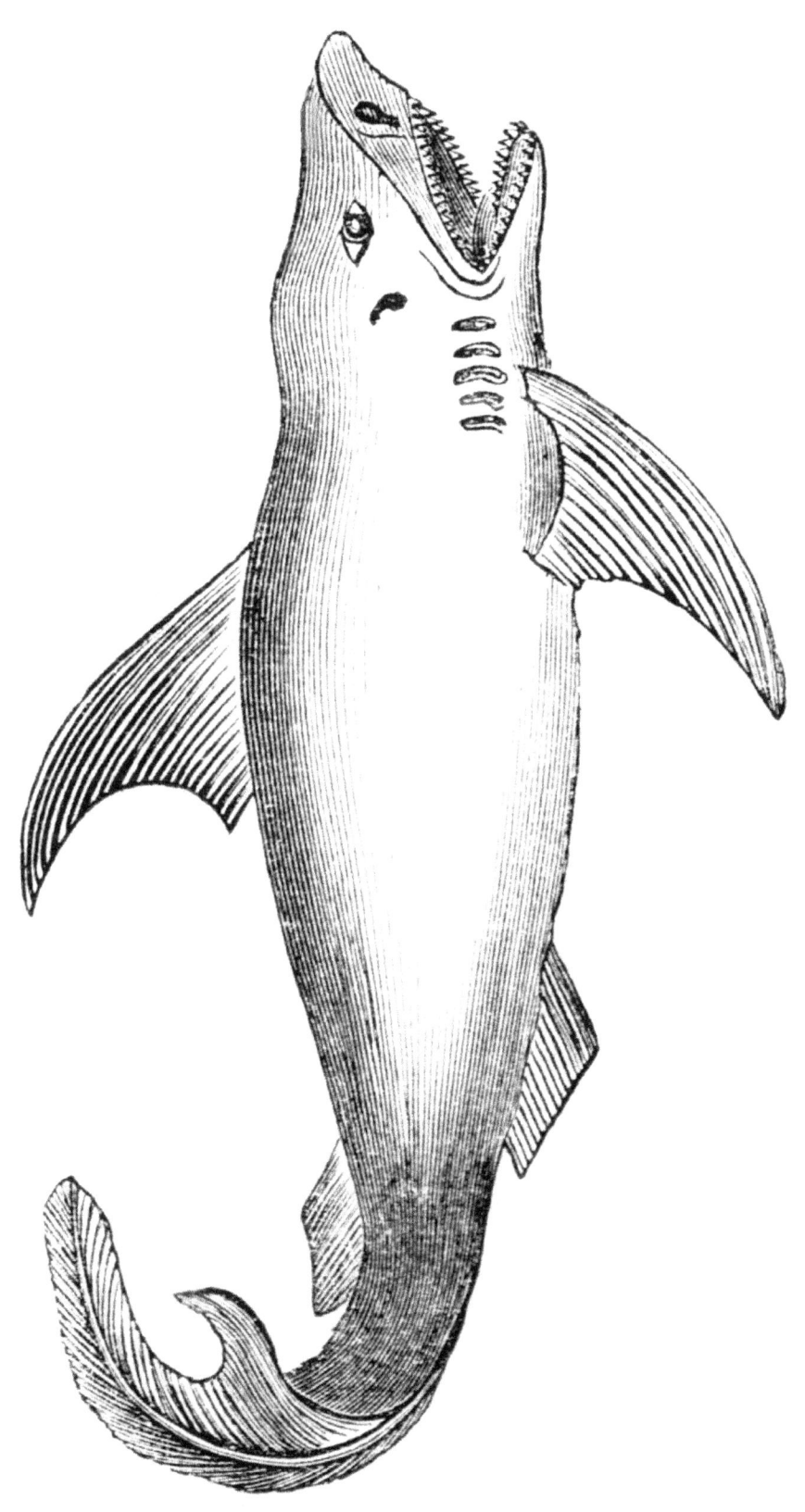

It was the sharpest, closest look I'd had at a great white shark's face and its alien head and the white underbelly of its throat, which was bulging, and at that moment it was as though time stopped.
—Susan Casey, *The Devil's Teeth* (2005)

WHITE SHARK

WHITECAPS

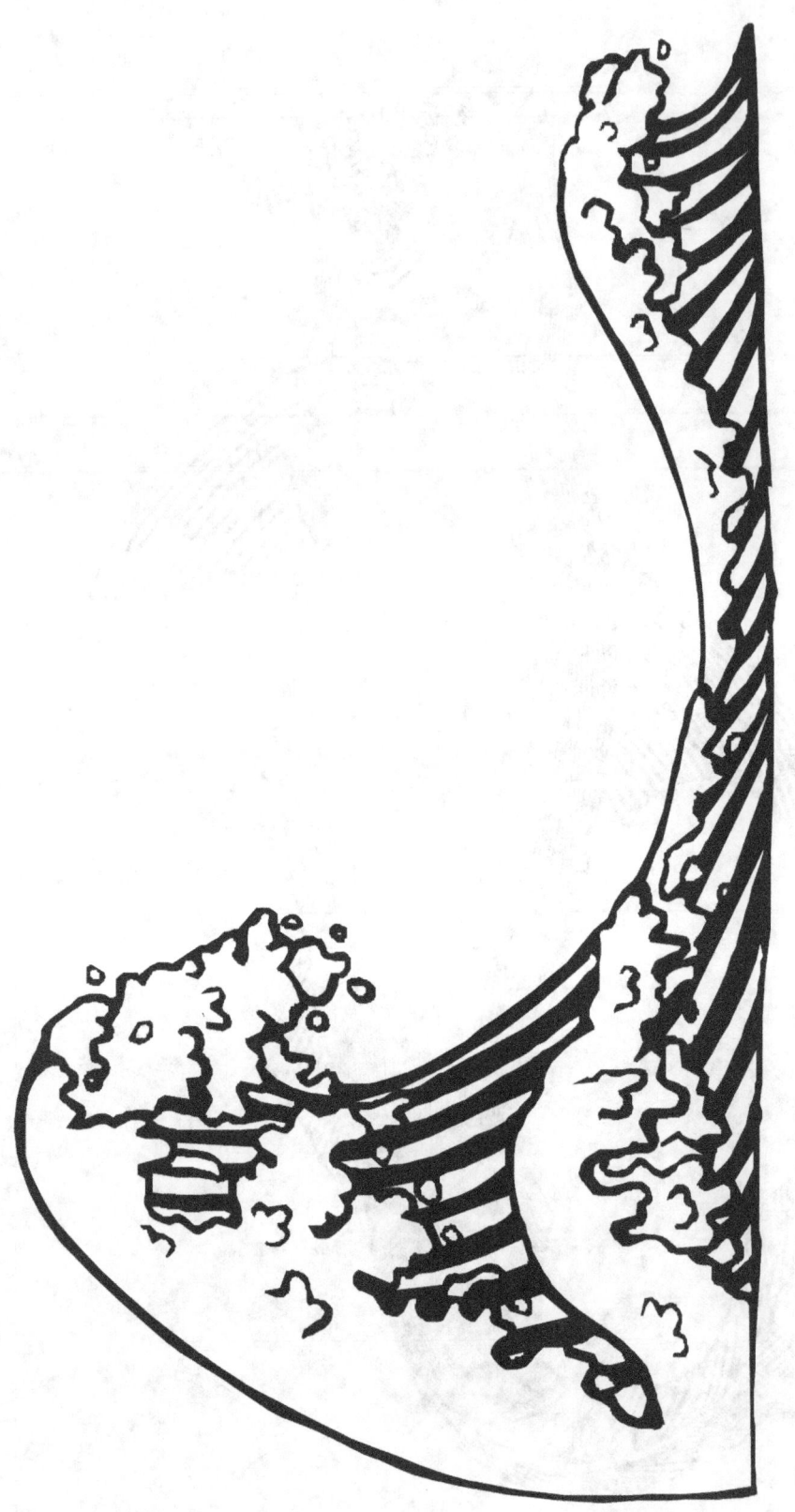

The sea stirred against the shore, leaving a long thin
curl of foam, white as a necklace of shells.
—Mary Mackey, *The Year the Horses Came* (2004)

MOBY DICK

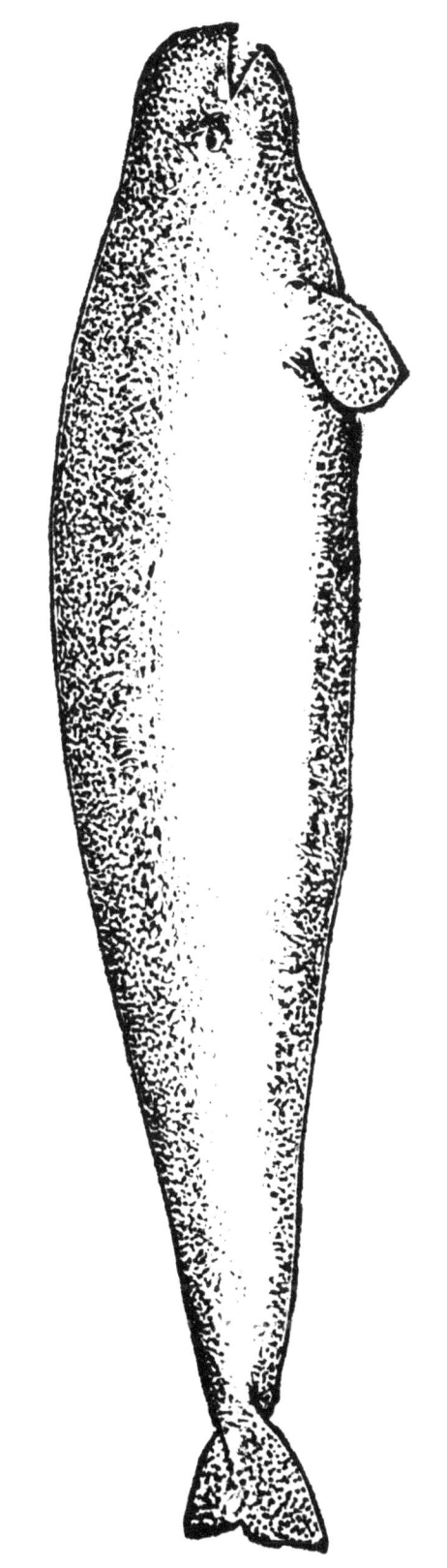

"Is it by its indefiniteness," Ishmael asks of "the whiteness of the whale,"
"it shadows forth the heartless voids and immensities of the universe?"
—Richard Gray, *A History of American Literature* (2004)

WHITE ASPARAGUS

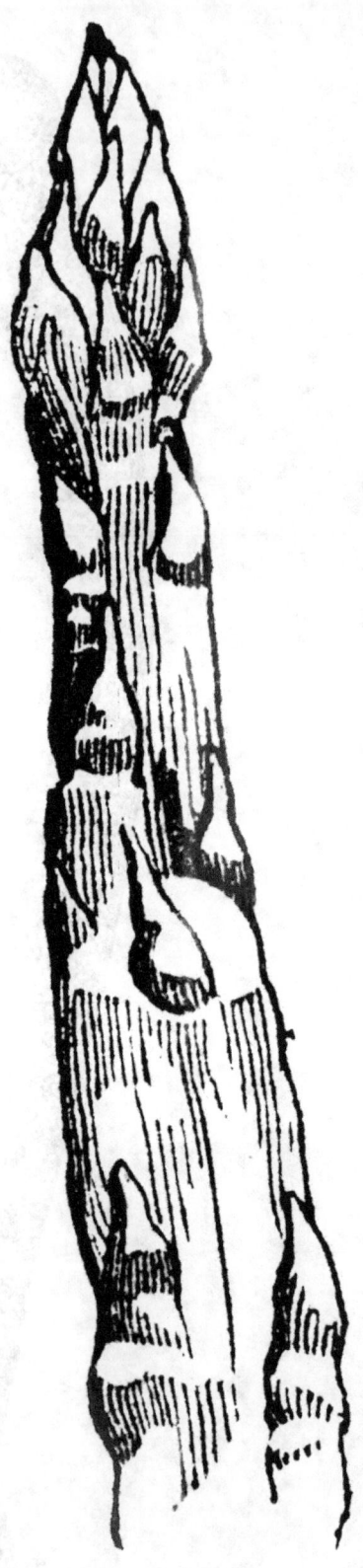

White asparagus is a peculiar thing.
—Gregg Wallace, *Veg: The Greengrocer's Cookbook* (2006)

WHITE CHEDDAR AND MILK

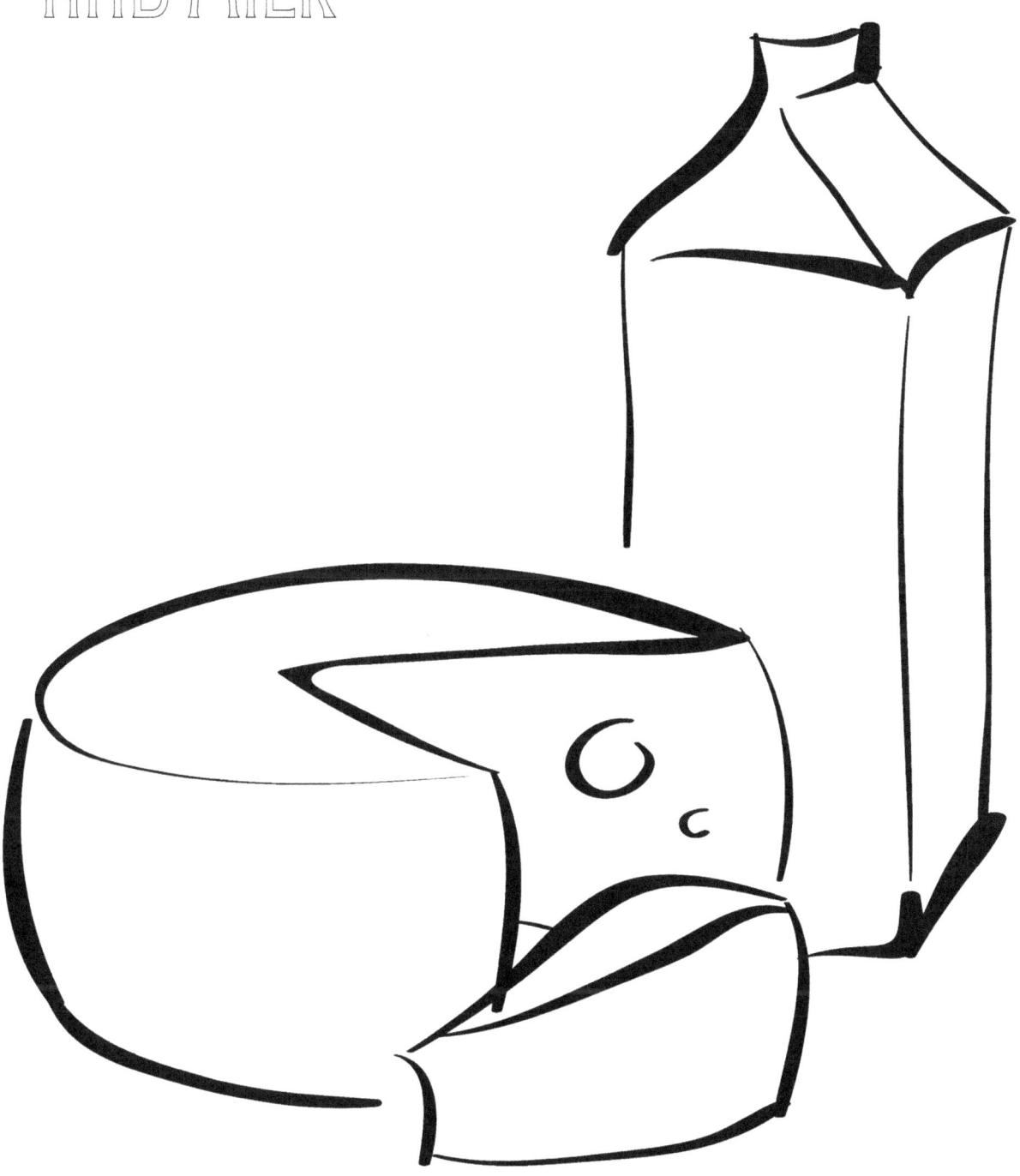

It looks like white cheddar. Could it be? I looked closer. I nearly squealed in delight.
—Lisa Bach, *Her Fork in the Road* (2001)

NOTEPAPER

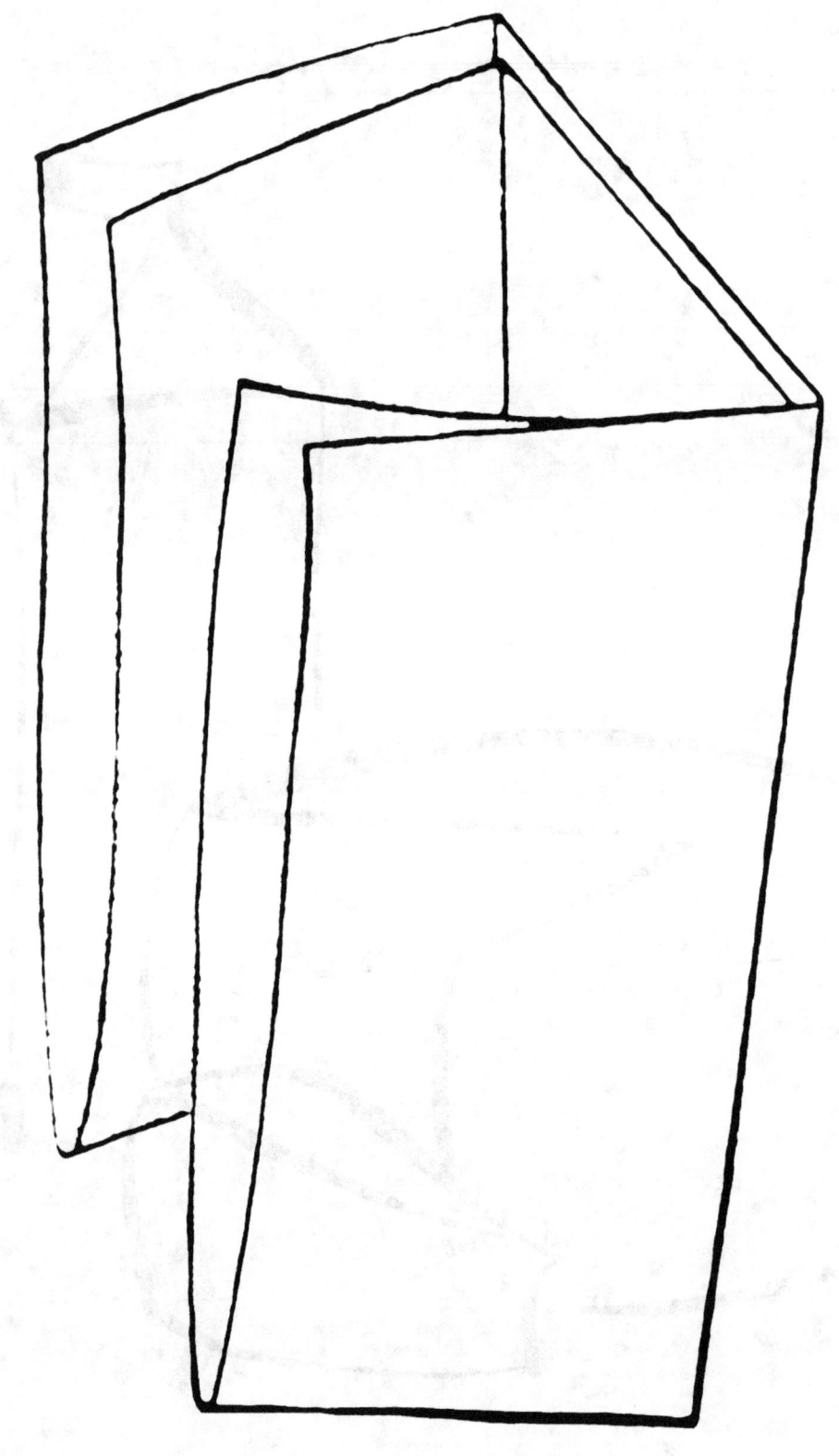

The other day, as I finished describing our meeting, I saw the blue ink marks on my white notepaper elude me, disappear.

—Françoise Sagan, *The Still Storm* (1986)

UGLY DUCKLINGS

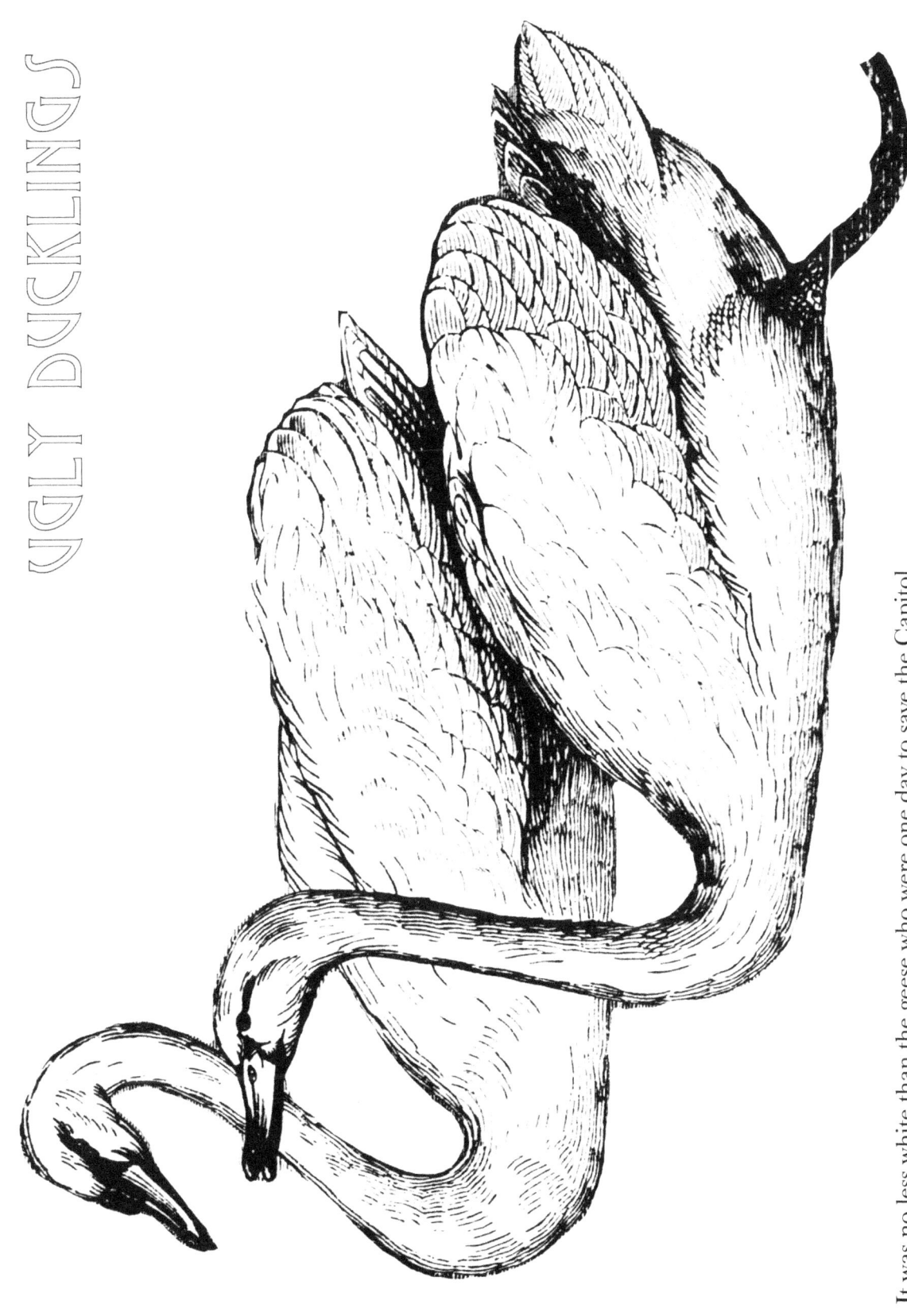

It was no less white than the geese who were one day to save the Capitol with their wakeful voices, as white as the swan that haunts rivers.

—Ovid, *Metamorphoses*

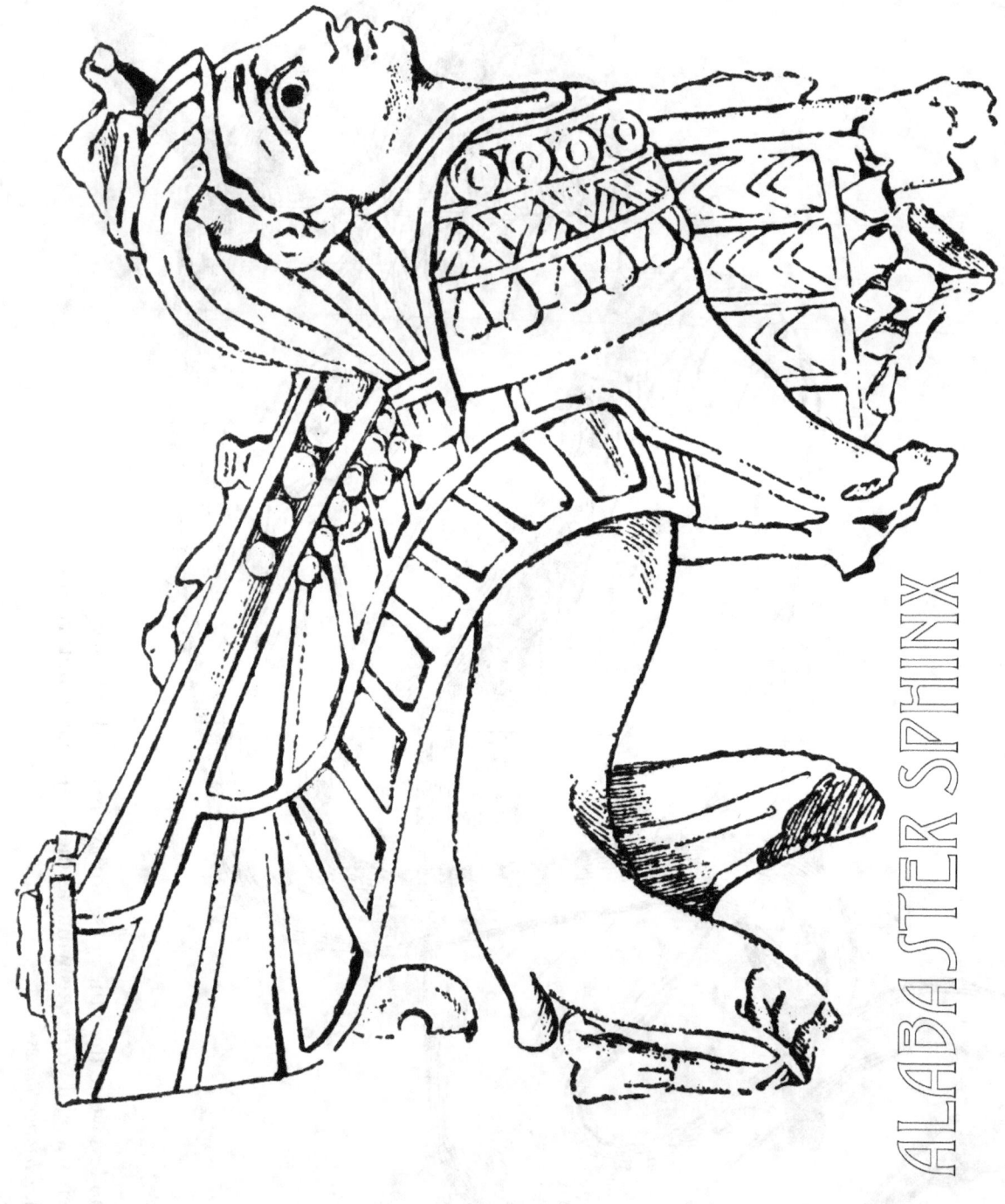

ALABASTER SPHINX

The desert west of Alexandria, where the sands were as white as alabaster, sparkling like salt.
—Margaret George, *The Memoirs of Cleopatra* (1997)

MILK VESSELS OF A DANDELION

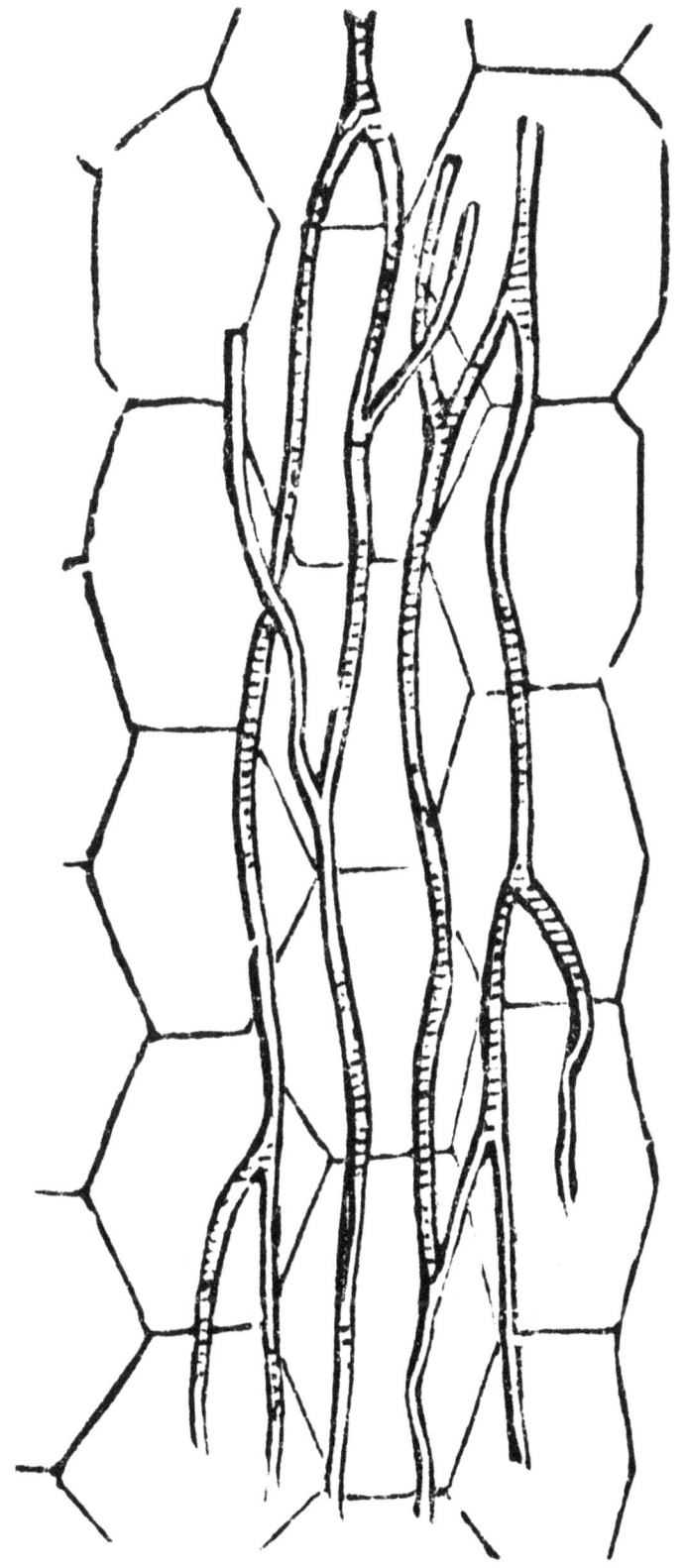

It has been sprinkled, one suspects, with no lustral water, but rather with the bitter milk of the common dandelion.

—Llewelyn Powus, "Milk of Dandelion" (1918)

GOLF BALL

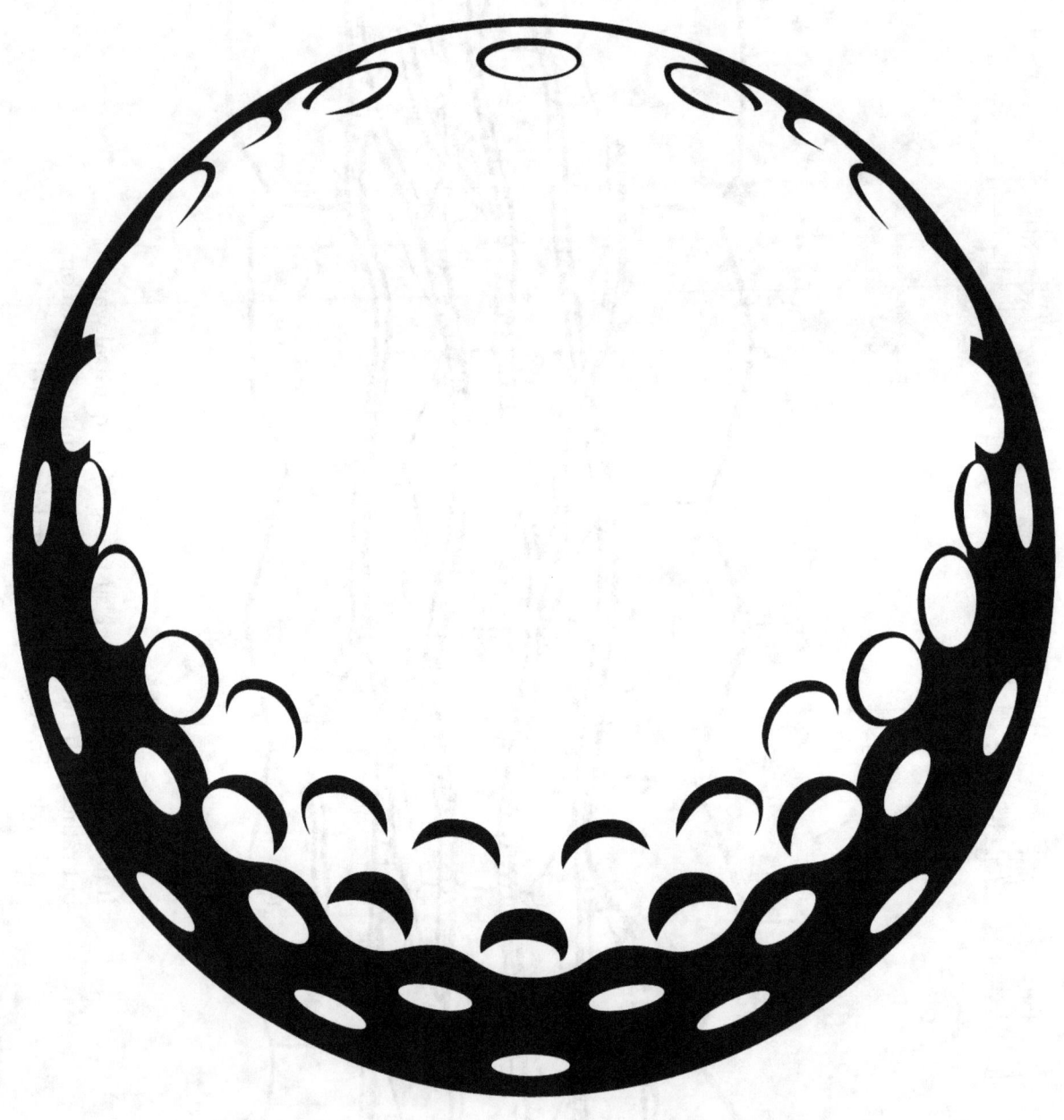

In the bright afternoon the reflection of the high moon
in the river had been small and white as a golf-ball.
—Frank Vigor Morley, *River Thames* (1926)

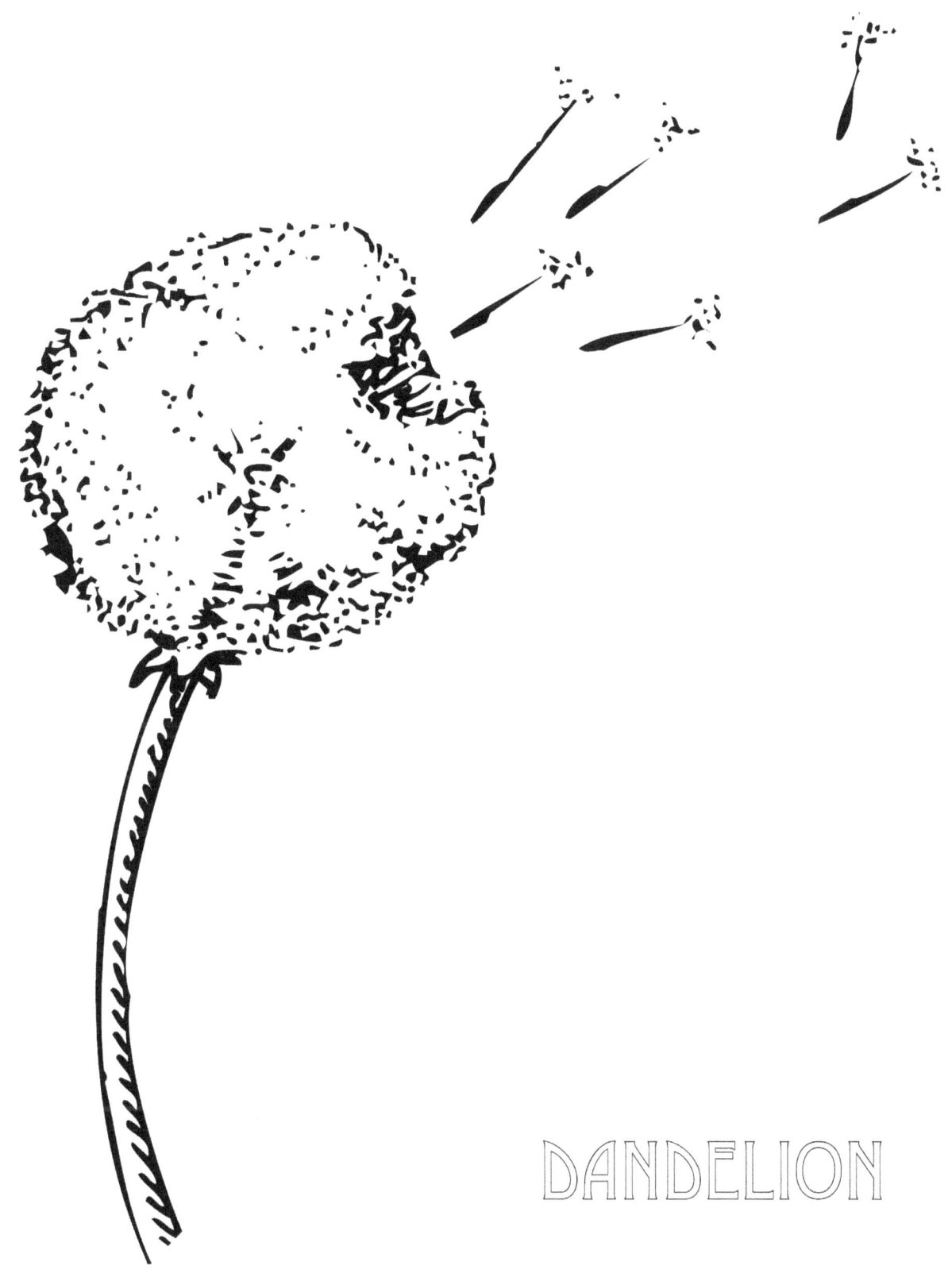

DANDELION

She was white as the downy spirit
Of the dandelion flower
—Henry Abbey, *The Poems of Henry Abbey* (1904)

WINTER

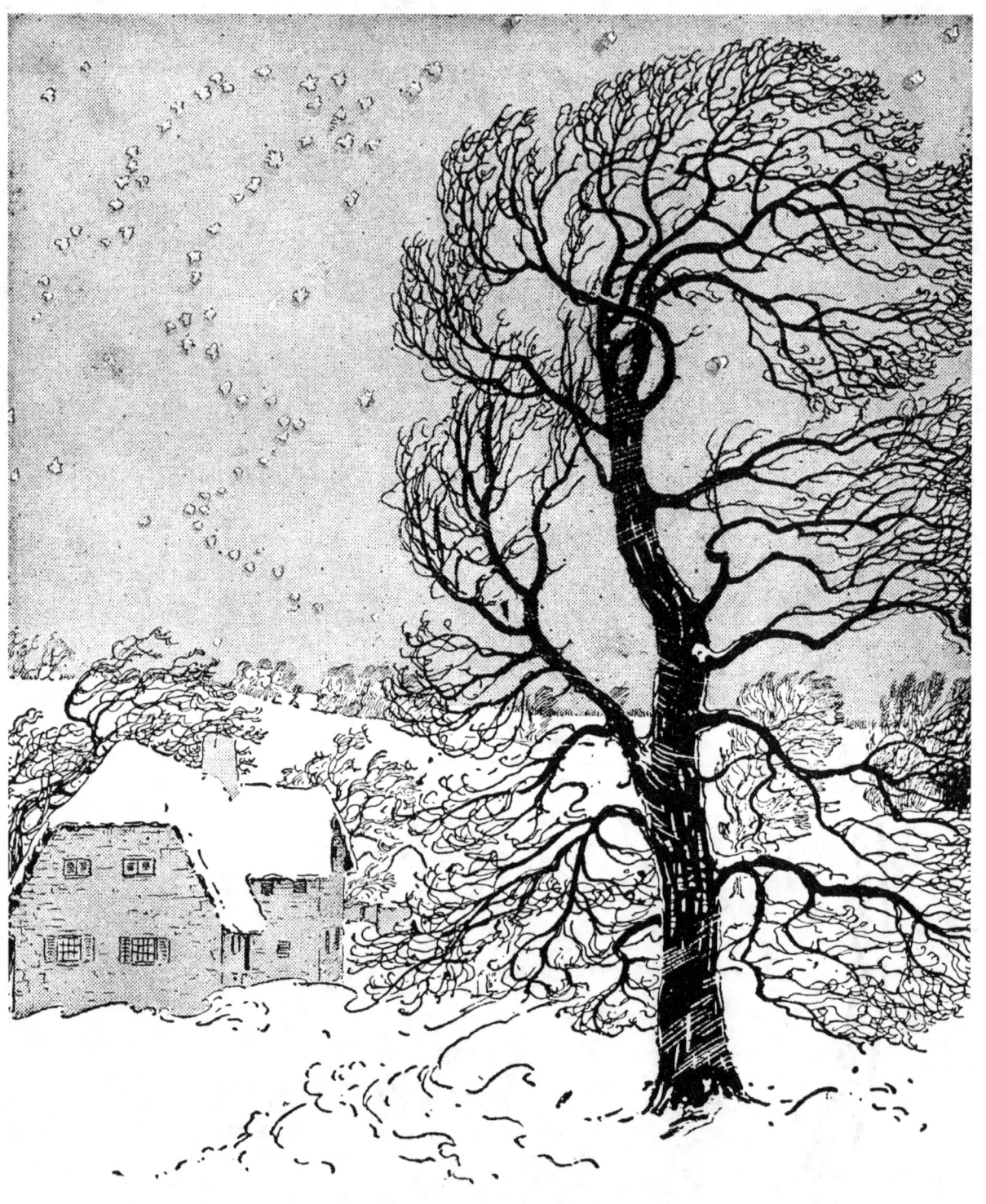

White as a winter home.
—John Payne

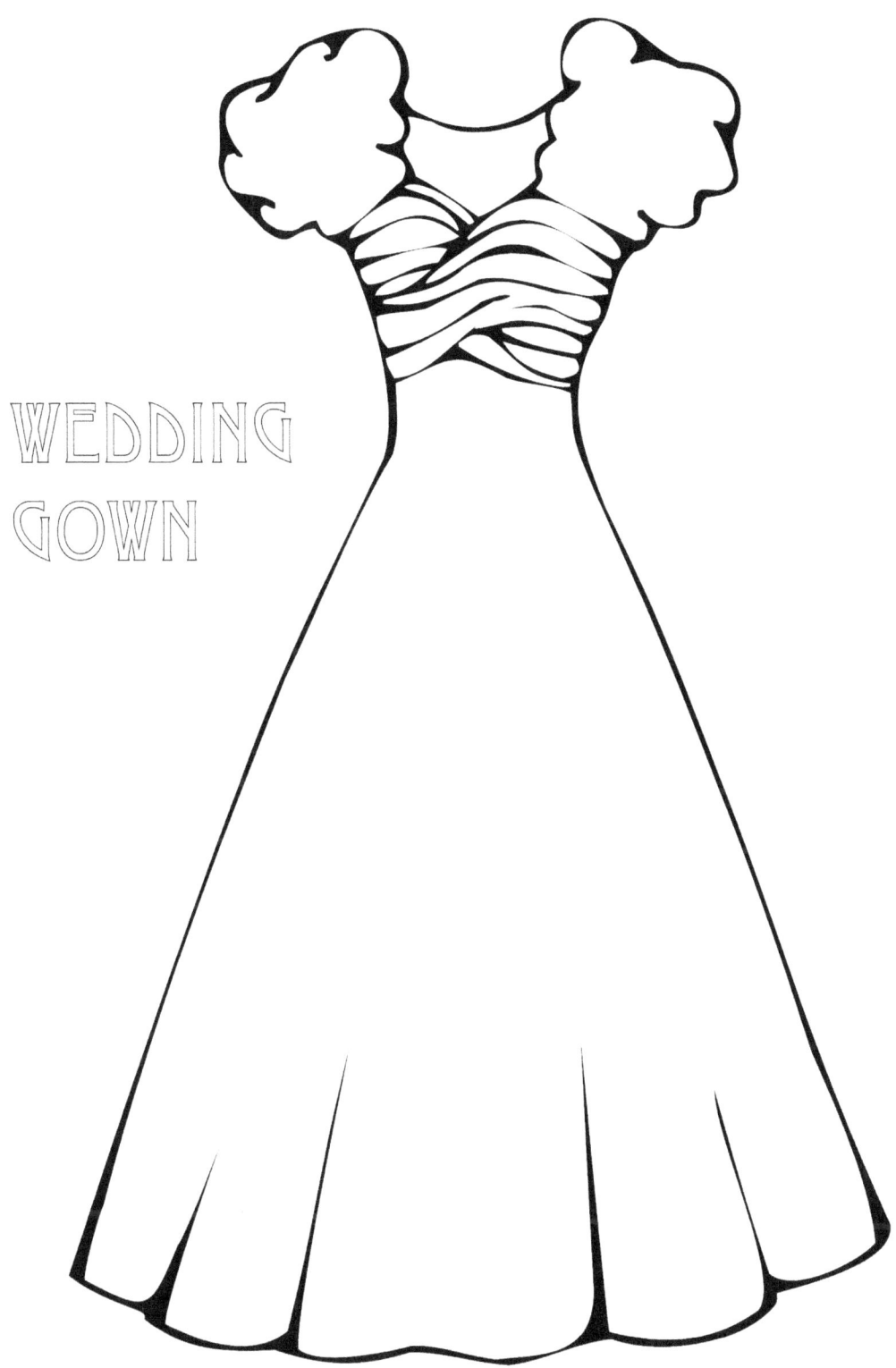

WEDDING
GOWN

My mother's wedding gown, still a crisp white as if it had just been returned by one of Picasso's stoop-shouldered ironing women from his blue period.
—Carlos Rojas, *The Garden of the Hesperides* (1999)

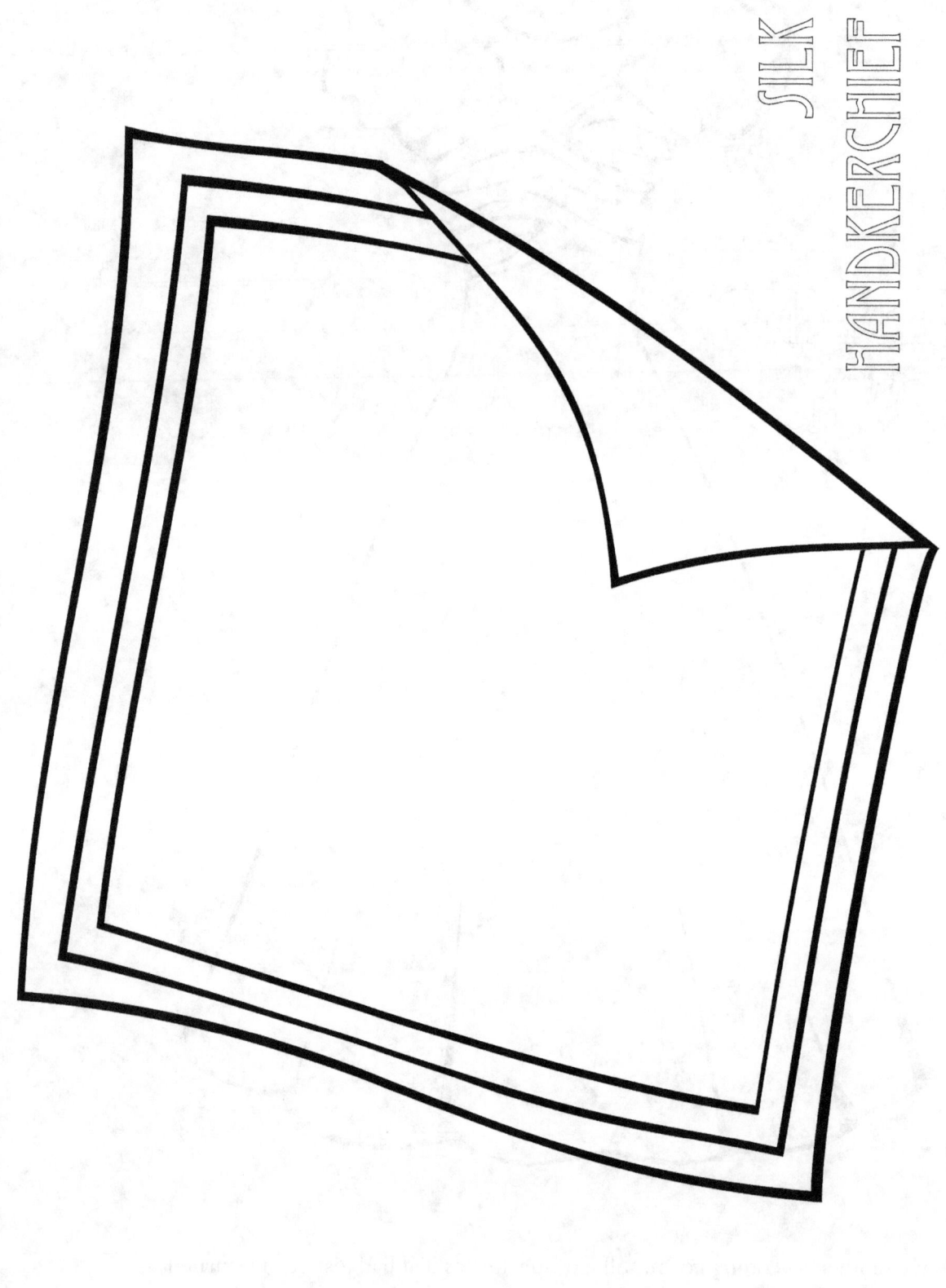

SILK
HANDKERCHIEF

Harry's hand was lady-like looking, and had once been white as the queen's cambric handkerchief.
—Herman Melville, *Redburn, His First Voyage* (1849)

ALBINO FERRET

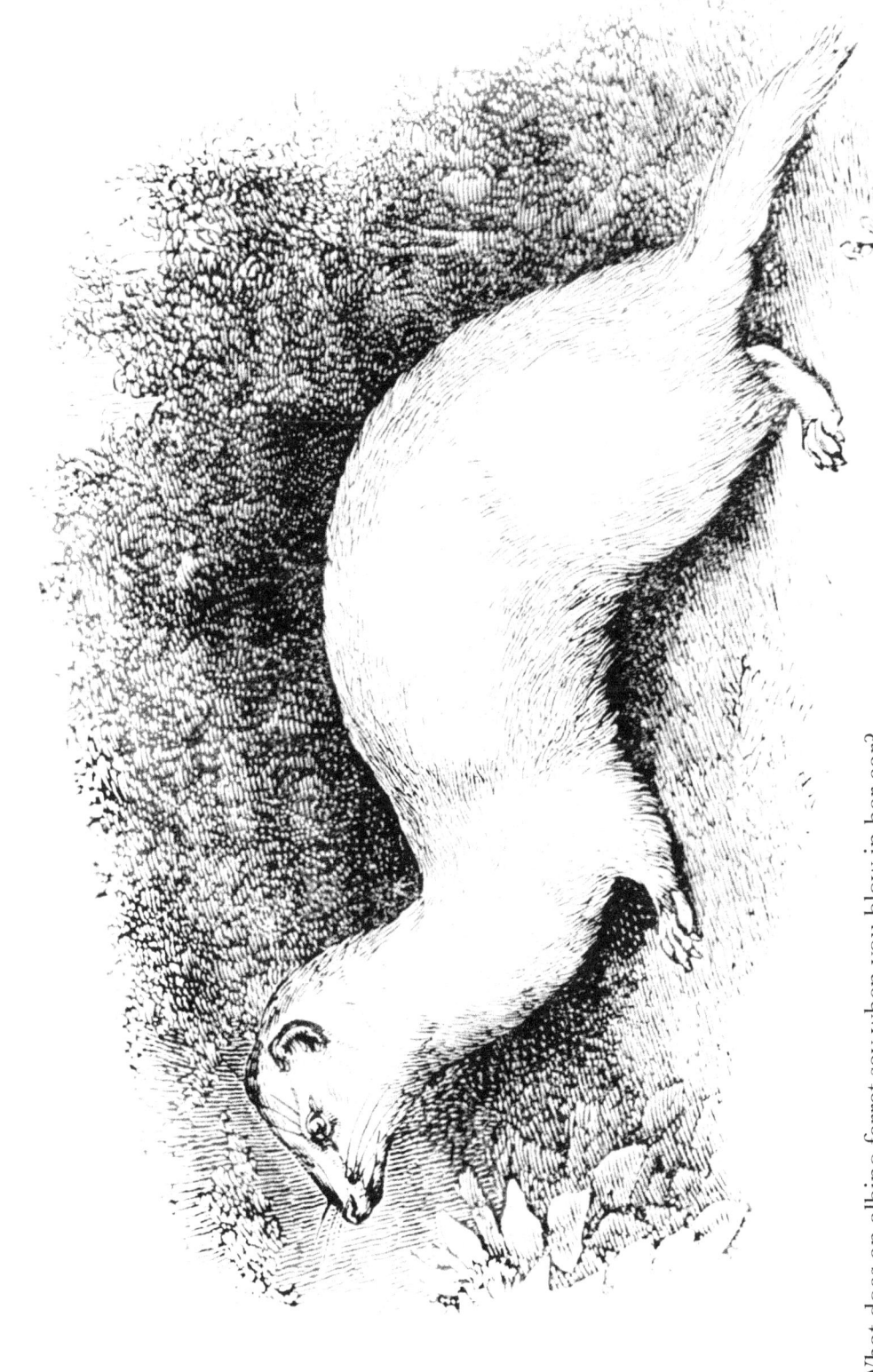

What does an albino ferret say when you blow in her ear?
"Thanks for the refill."
—Richard Bach, *Air Ferrets Aloft* (2002)

BIB

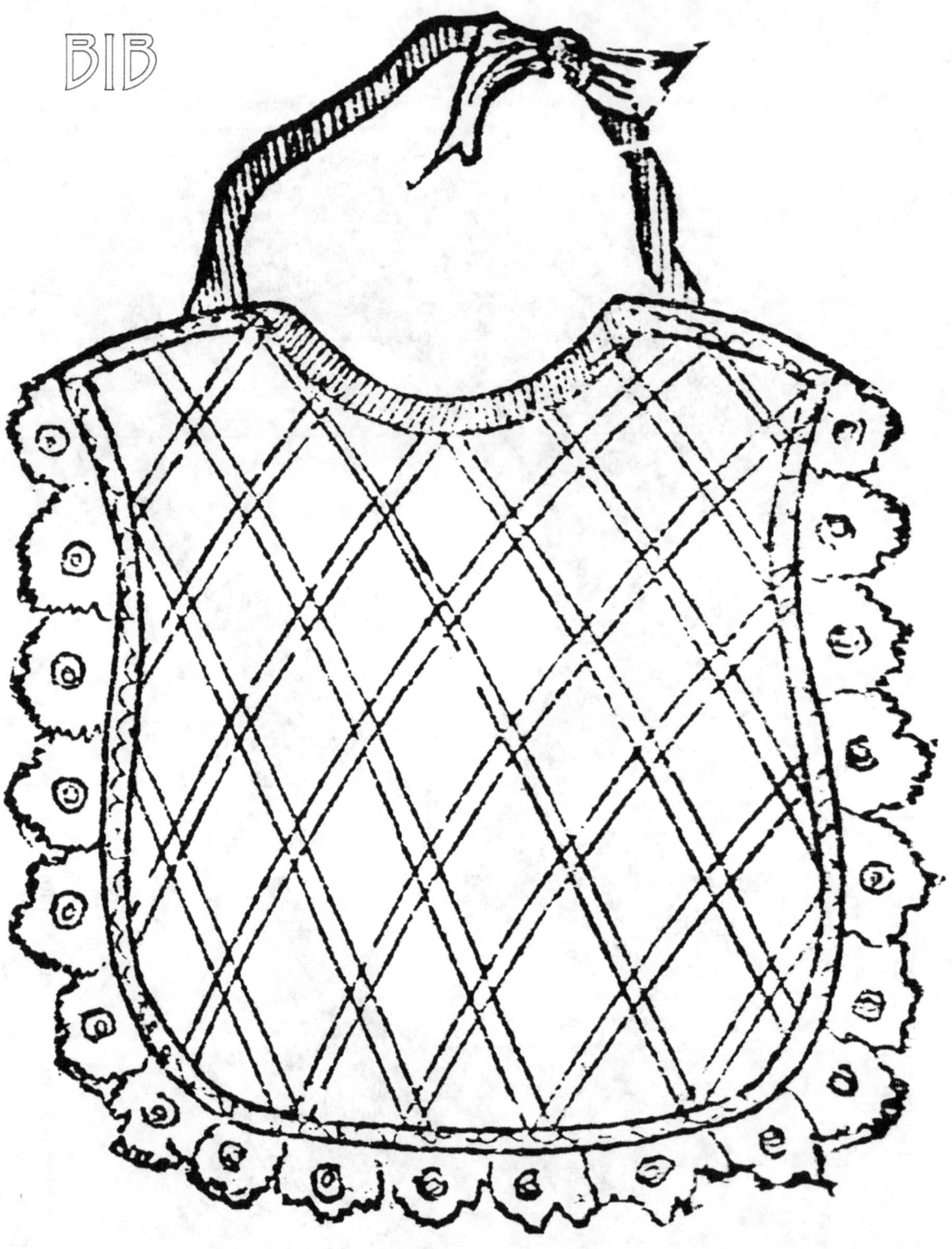

She wore . . . a fiercely white bib-apron and collar, and a white linen cap
with two broad white streamers floating from it down to the waist.
—Thomas Burke, *Son of London* (1946)

MILK FAT (MAGNIFIED)

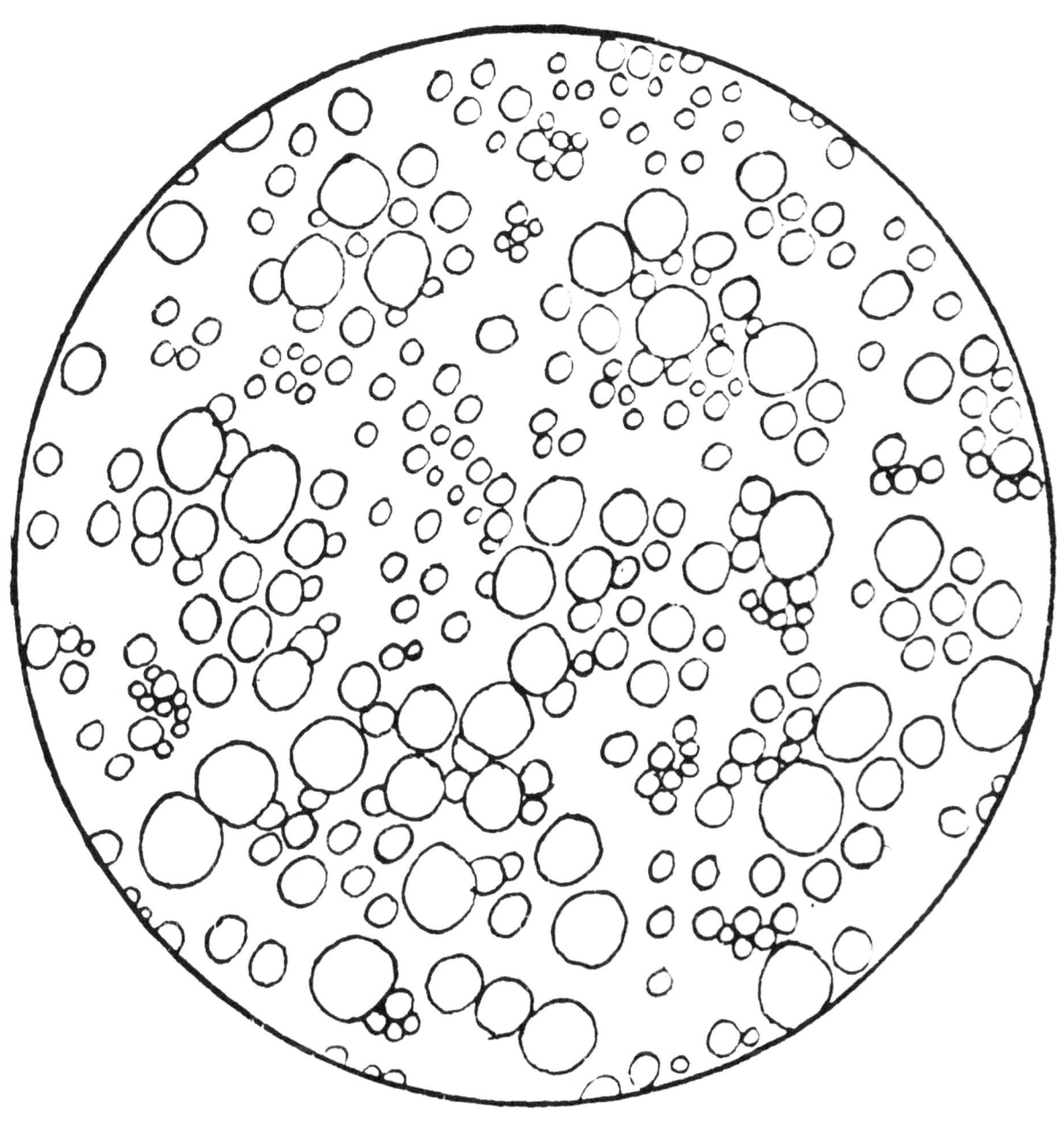

The smaller are the globules, the whiter is the milk.
—Paul Gustav Heinemann, *Milk* (1919)

YORICK

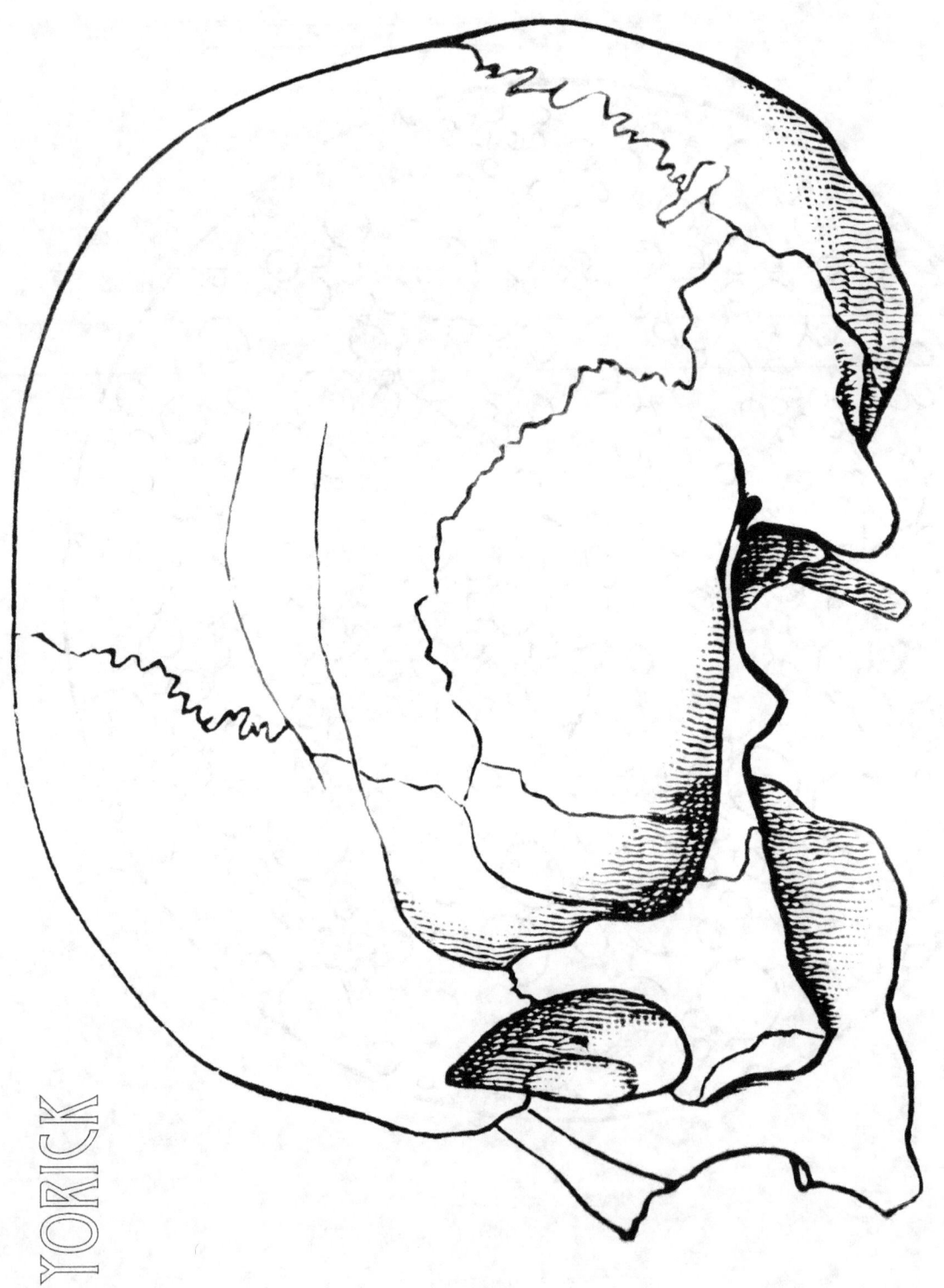

He walked slowly into the middle of the clearing and looked steadily at the skull that gleamed as white as ever the conch had done and seemed to jeer at him cynically.
—William Golding, *Lord of the Flies* (1954)

BLANK CHECK

No. _____

CHICAGO, ILLS. _____

FORT DEARBORN NATIONAL BANK

Pay to the order of _____

$ _____

_____ DOLLARS

Does this look too much like a blank check?

—*Record of Christian Work* (1919)

ANGEL FOOD CAKE

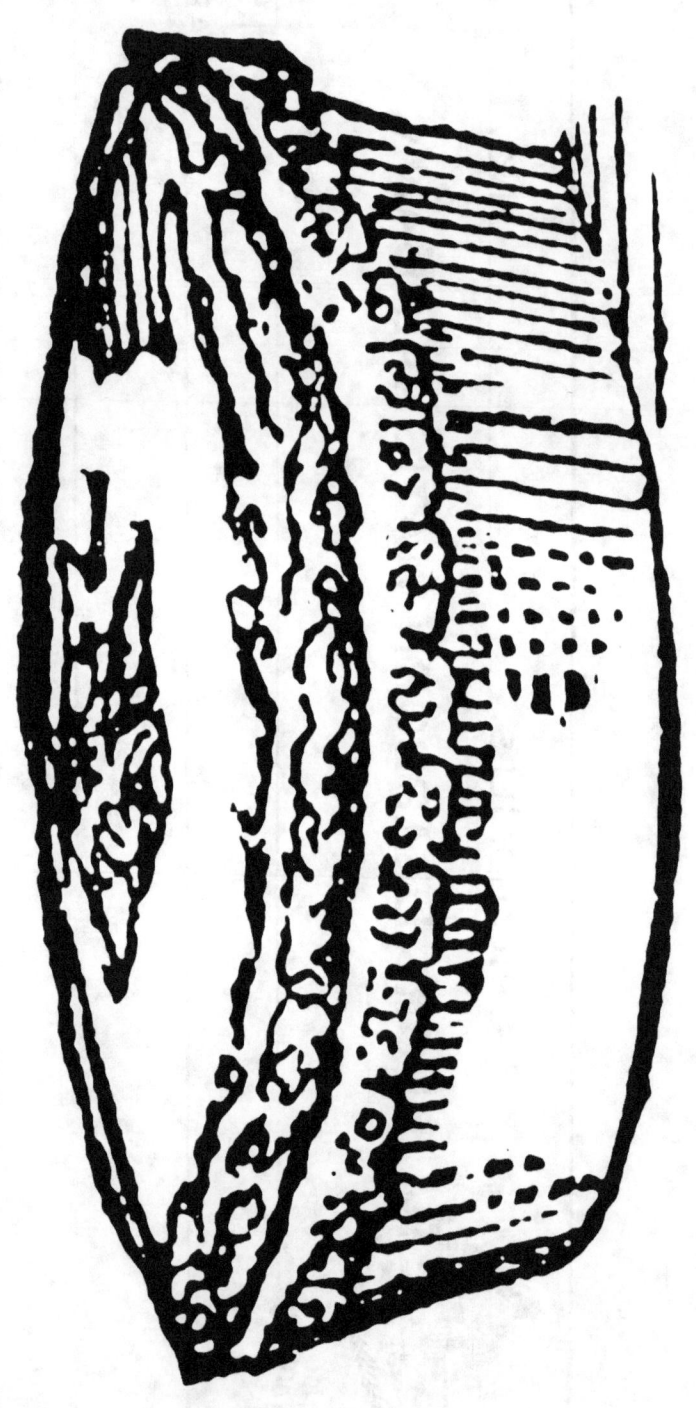

It was an angel food cake with an icing as white and light and swirly as a summer cloud. It was as white as a bride. The sight of it fairly took his breath—it was the most delicate and wondrous thing that he had ever seen.
—Wendell Berry, *That Distant Land* (1908)

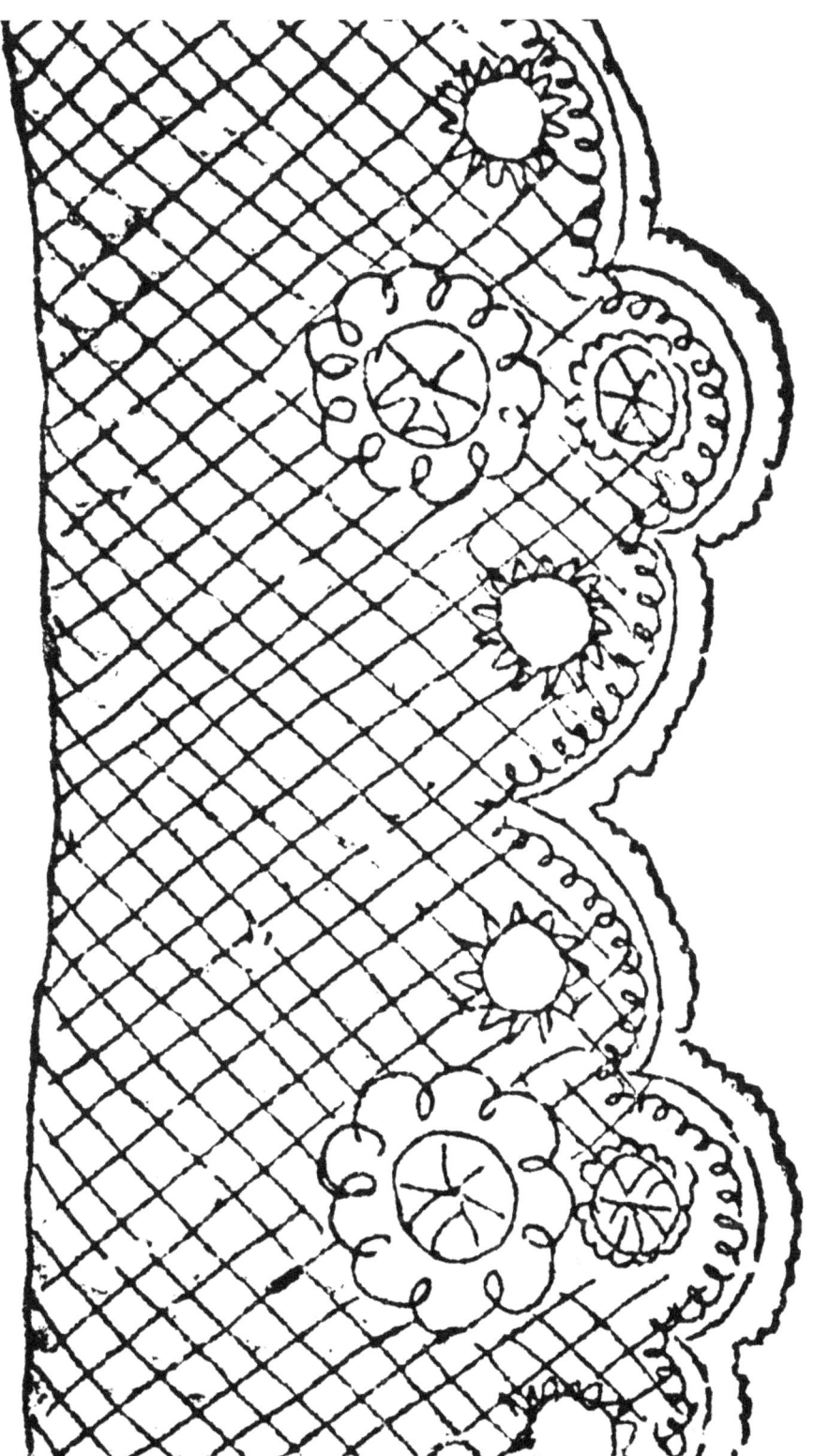

LACE

White as lace, delicate as unfolding insect wings.
—Robert Bly, *Iron John* (1990)

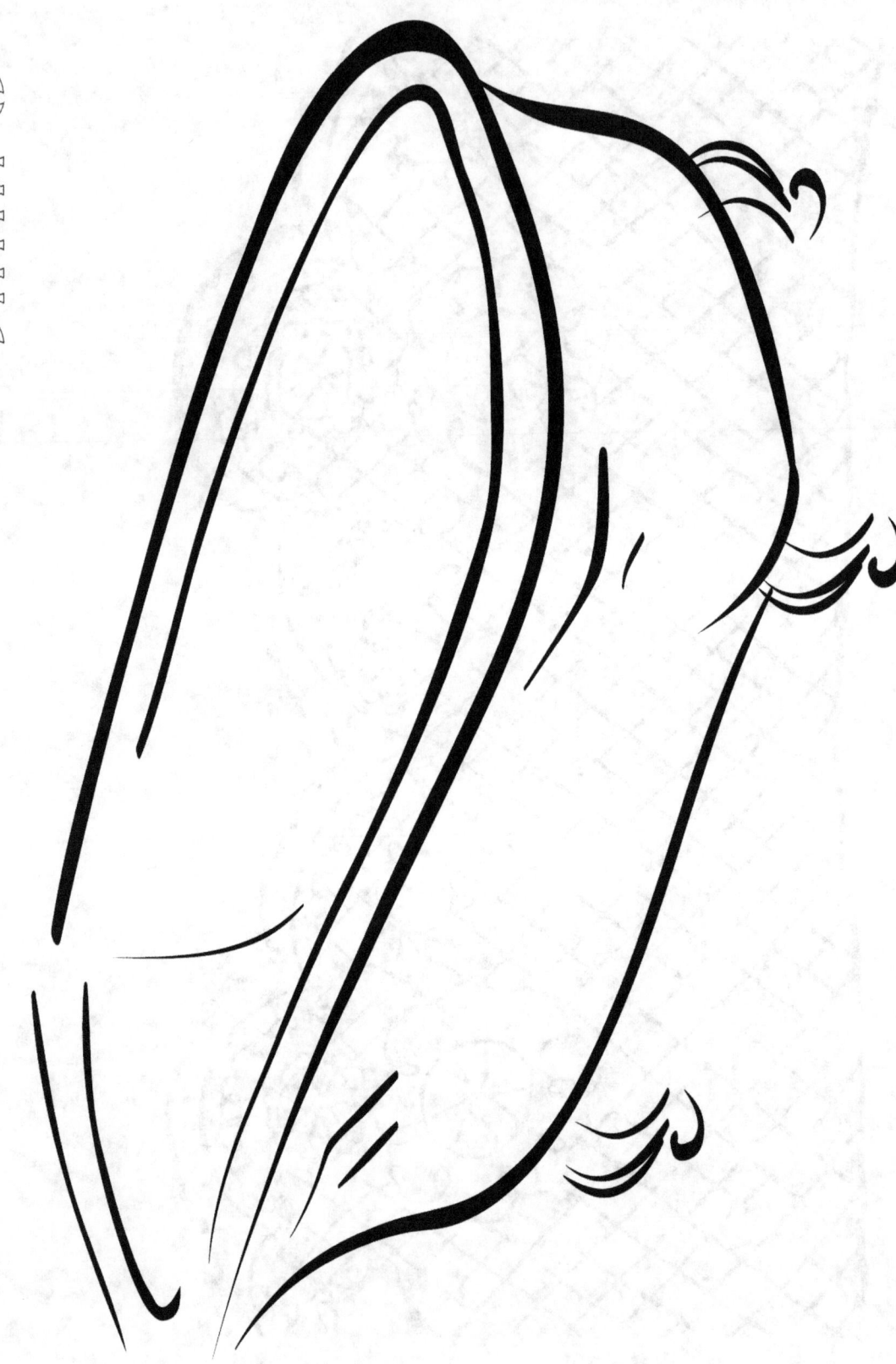

White as a bathtub and glittering.
—Whit Burnett, *Story* (1931)

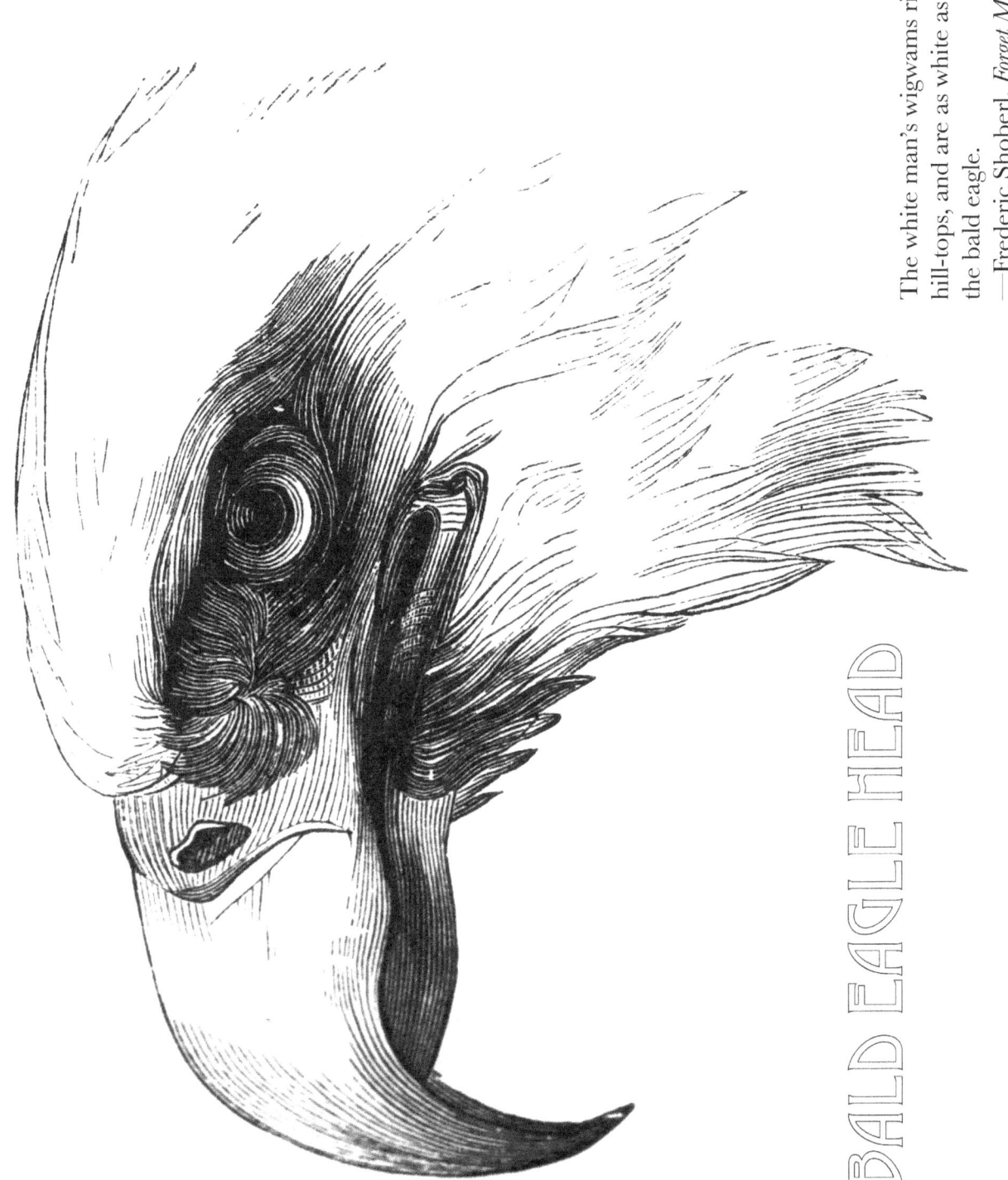

The white man's wigwams rise like the hill-tops, and are as white as the head of the bald eagle.

—Frederic Shoberl, *Forget Me Not* (1847)

BALD EAGLE HEAD

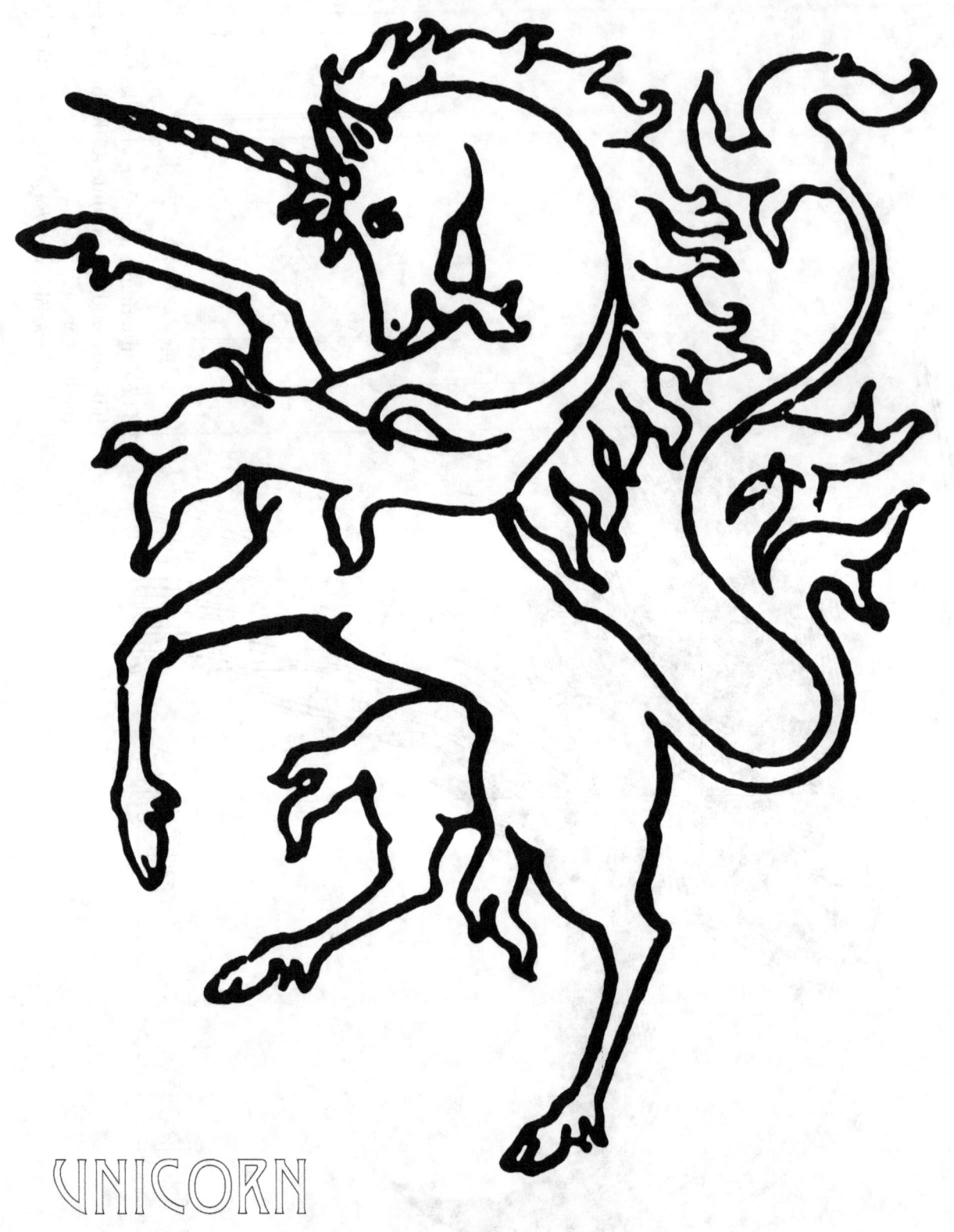

UNICORN

Not as white as a unicorn, of course, but nearly.
—Mercedes Lackey, *To Light a Candle* (2004)

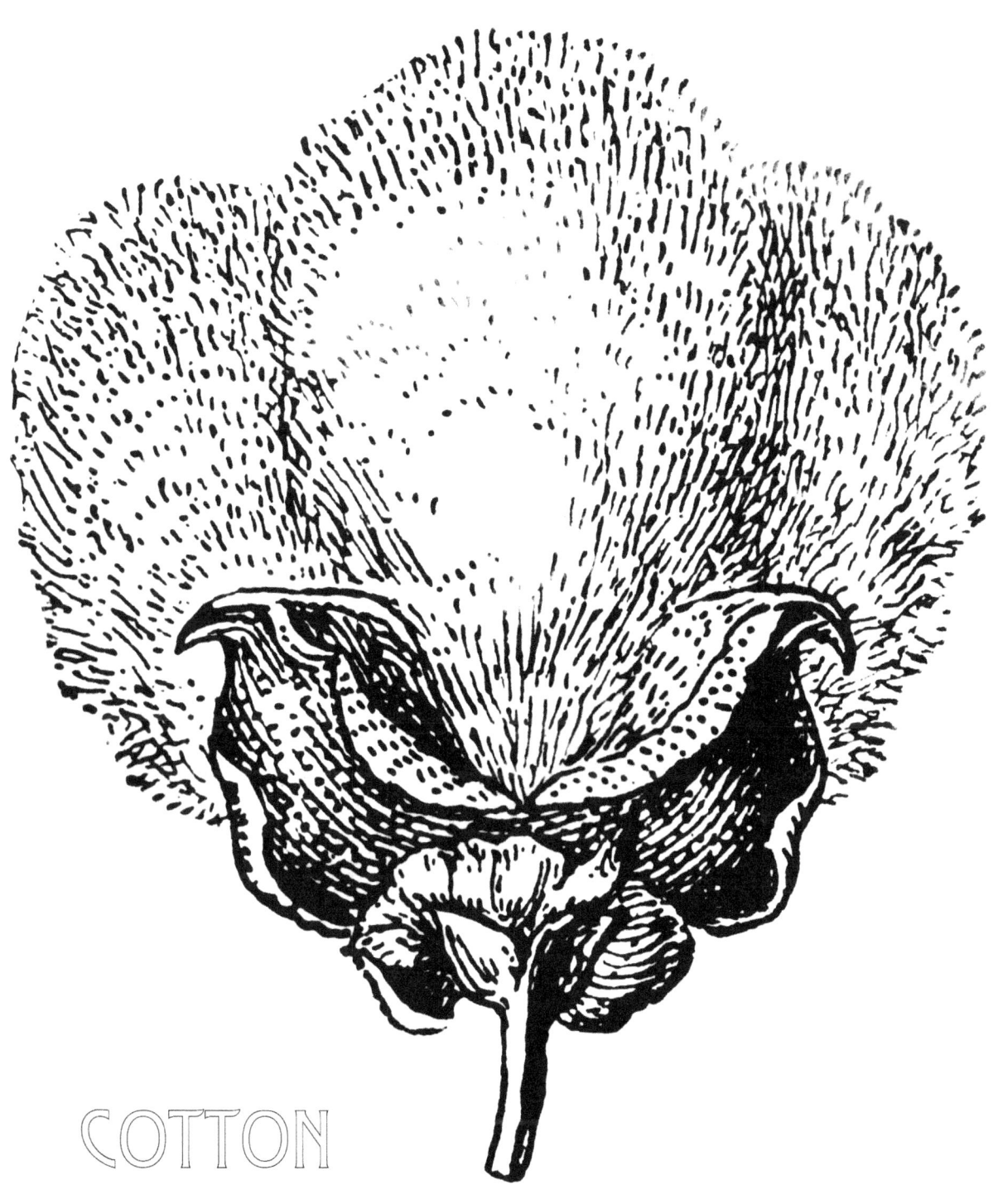

COTTON

The cotton thread was bleached by placing it on a line in the yard, where it hung for two or three weeks in the sun and dew. . . . Such thread would bleach almost as white as snow.
—Parthenia Antoinette Hague, *A Blockaded Family* (1888)

GREEK TEMPLE

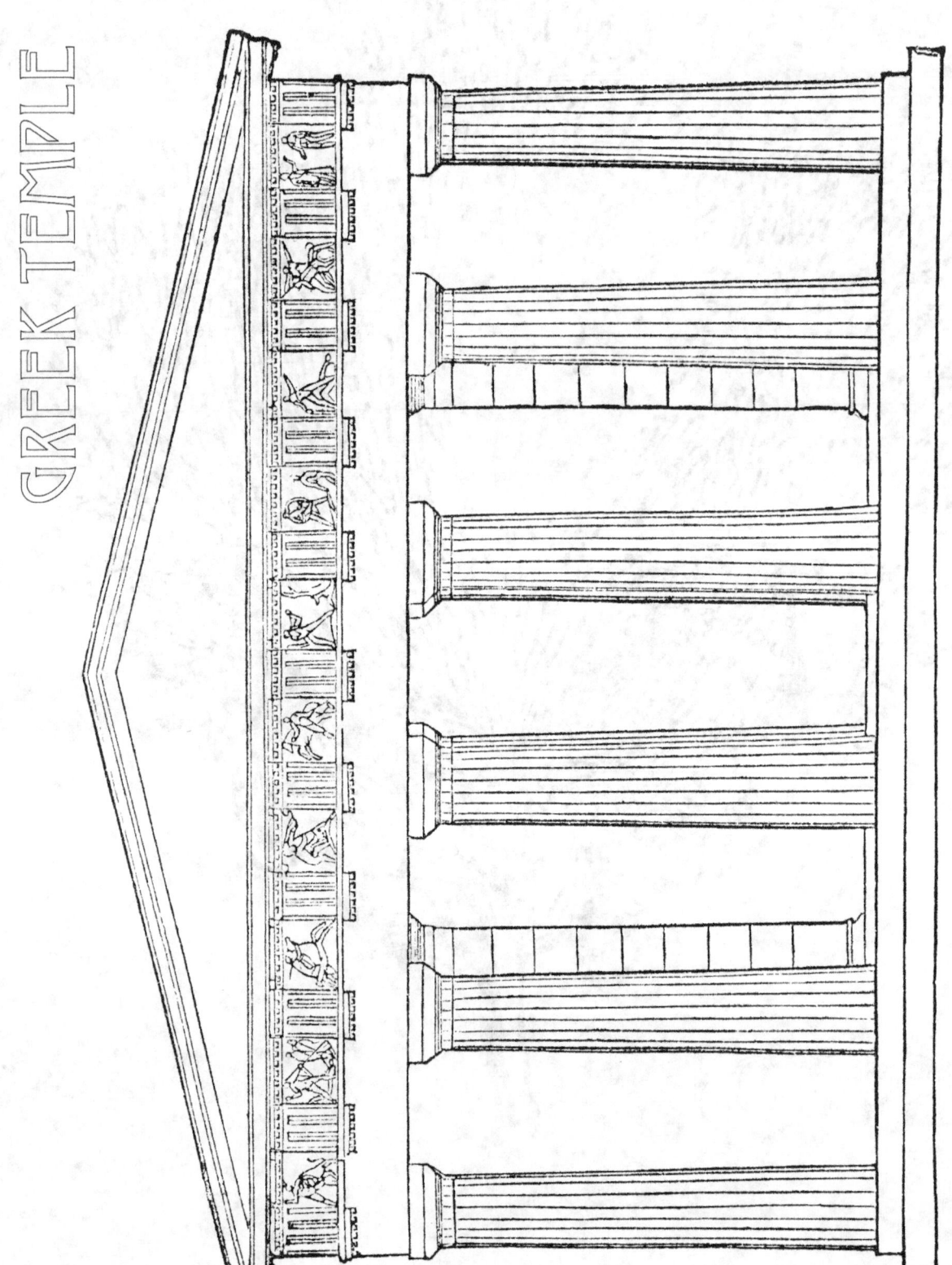

She was white as the marble pillar near which she stood, and apparently as insensible to what was passing around her.
—Rhoda Elizabeth Waterman White, *Mary Staunton* (1860)

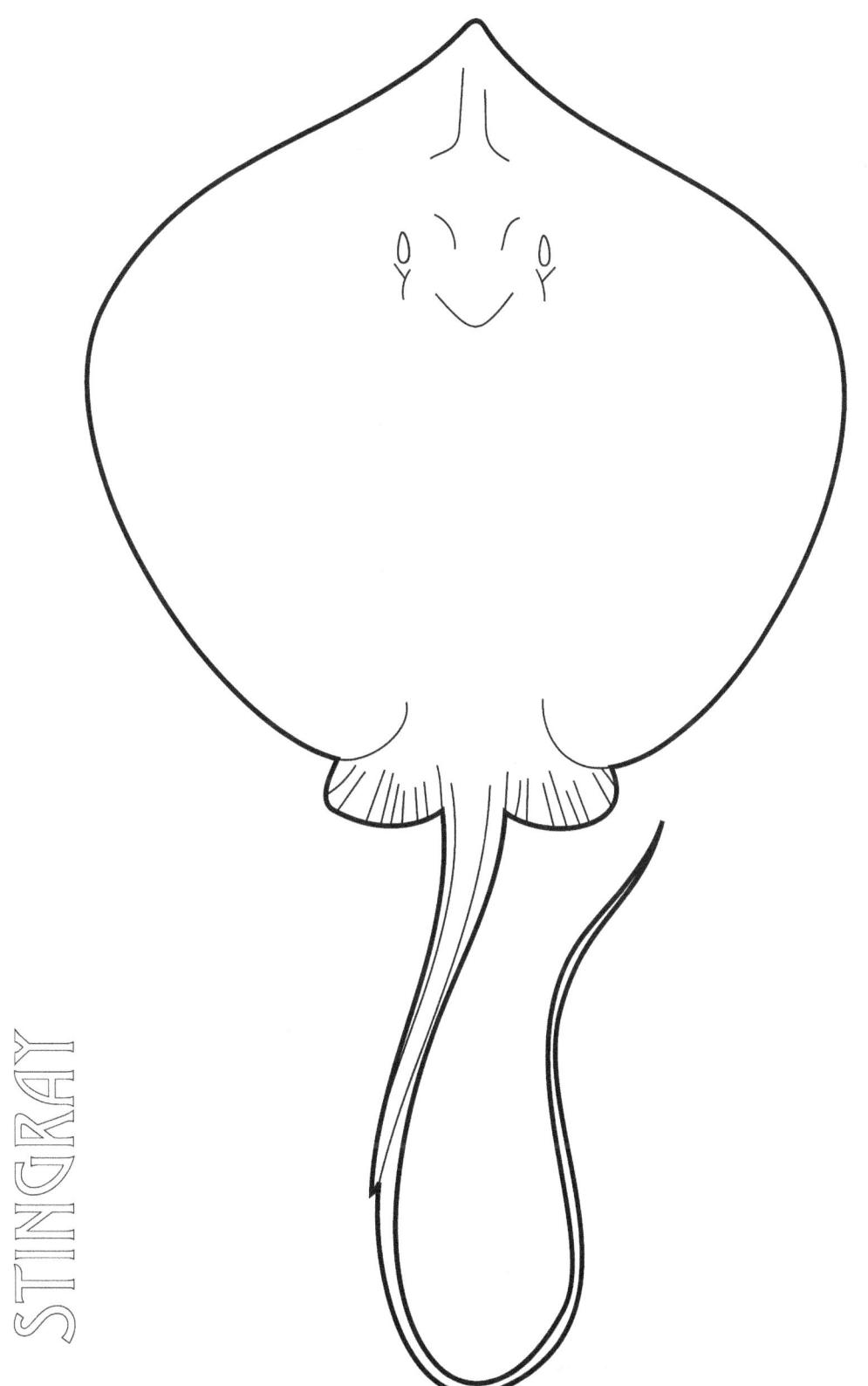

STINGRAY

That's not a white light. It's an albino stingray. He's a hero, but we have to get him back into the water.
—Rhea Perlman, *Water Balloon Doom* (2006)

HARPSICHORD SHARPS

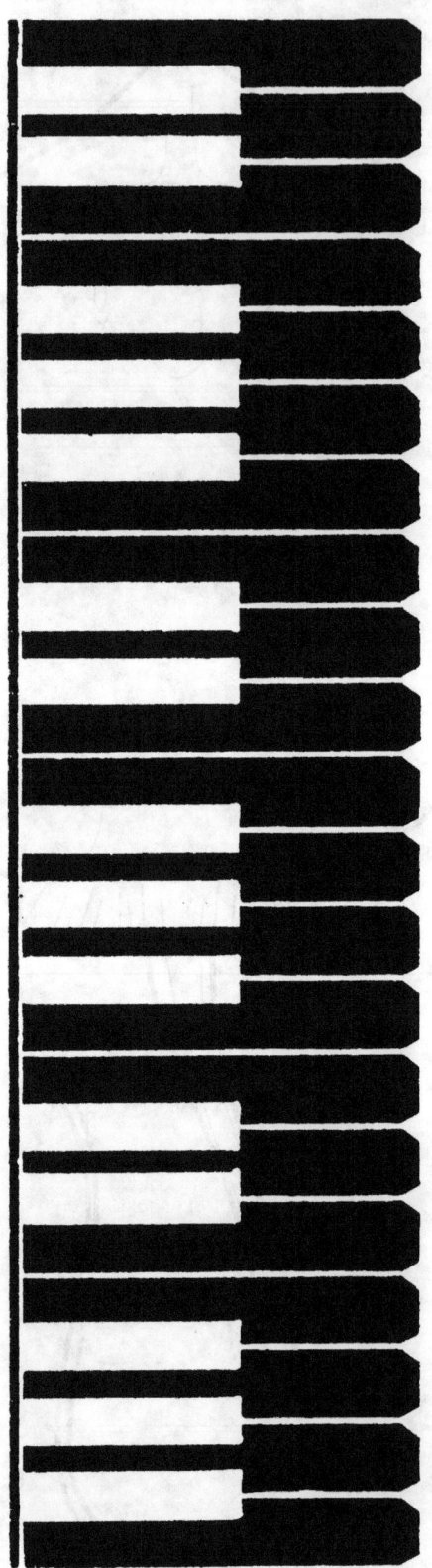

The keys white in a piano were in this case black, and those usually black were white.
—Martim de Albuquerque, *Notes and Queries* (1879)

PIANO NATURALS

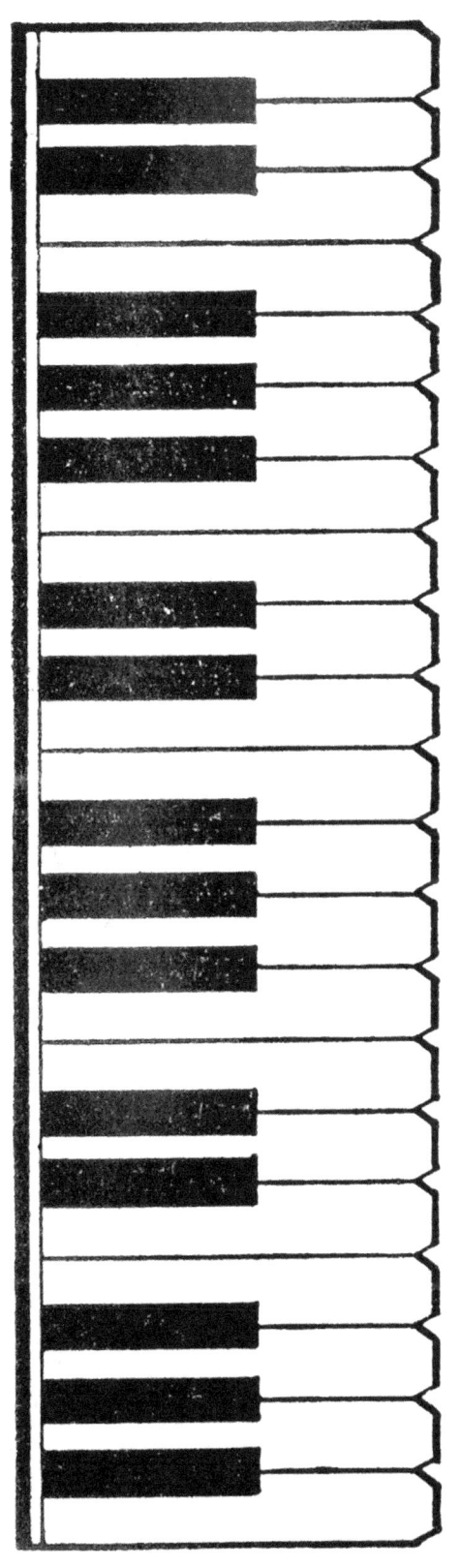

I was freshly painted white fence spokes and ivory piano keys.

—Kate Braverman, *Lithium for Medea* (1979)

IGLOOS

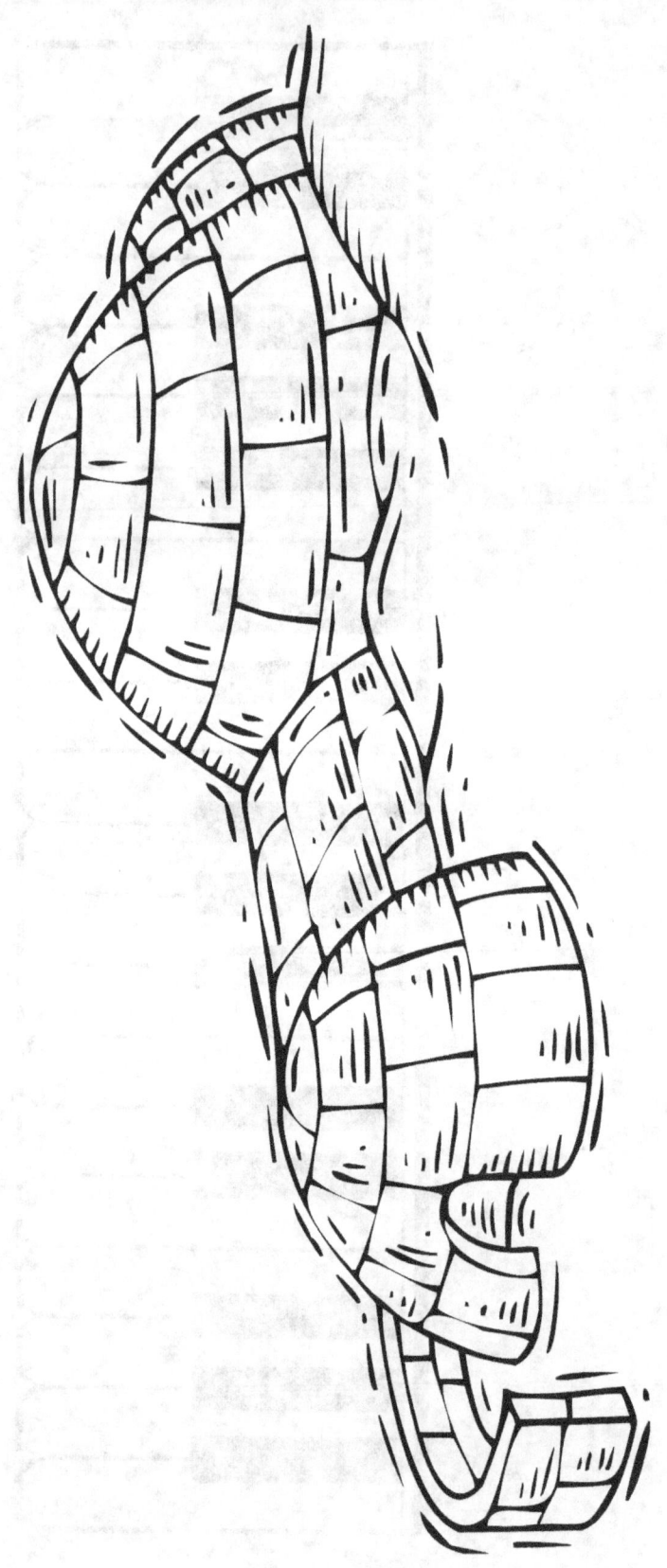

I paint your igloos and your hunting-grounds as white as my face
so that you should find your way in the long winter night.
—Henry Beissel, *Inuk and the Sun* (1980)

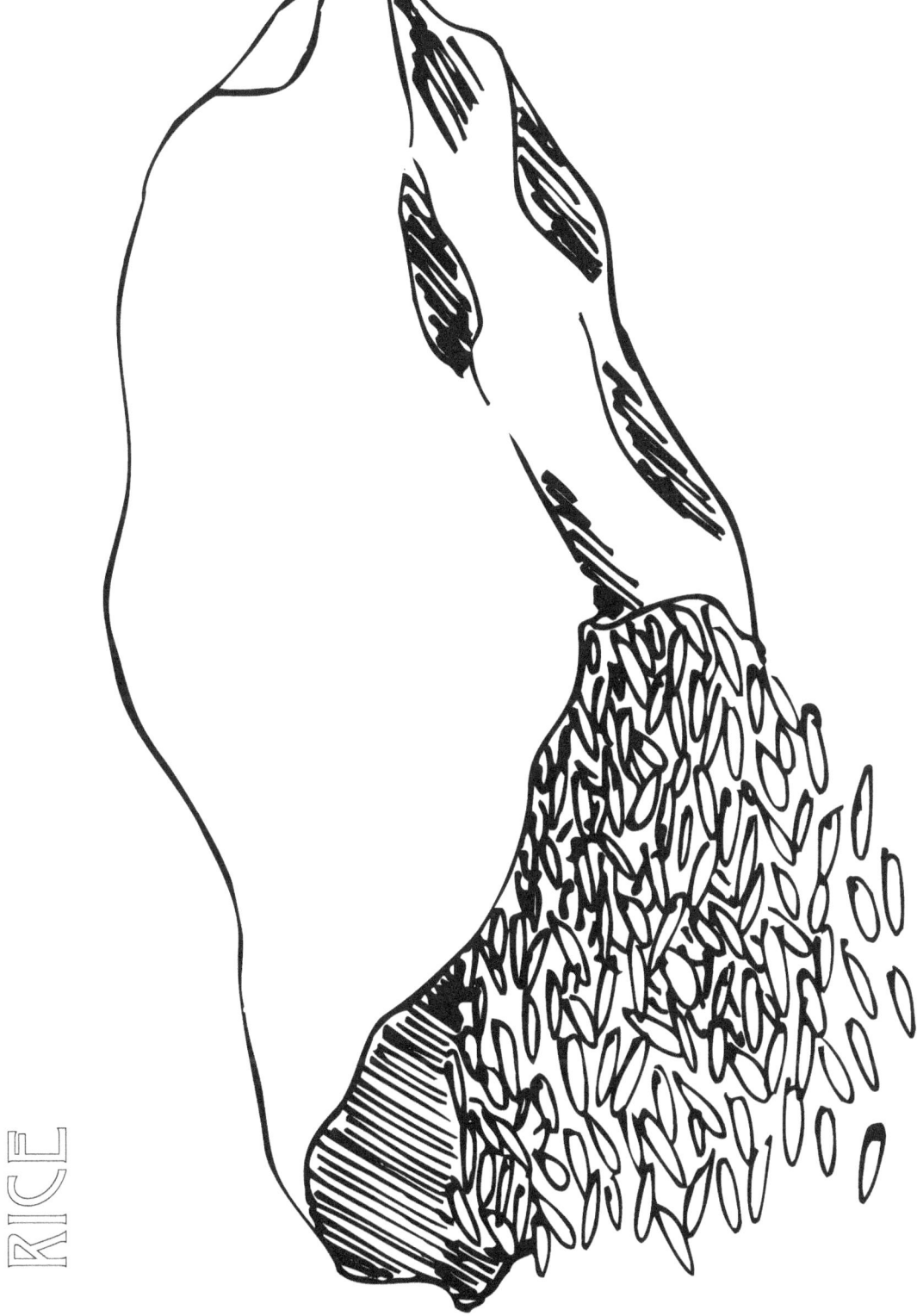

RICE

Very few white organisms are as white as white rice but nothing would be gained by calling all of them chromogens.

—Erwin Frink Smith, *Introduction to Bacterial Diseases of Plants* (1920)

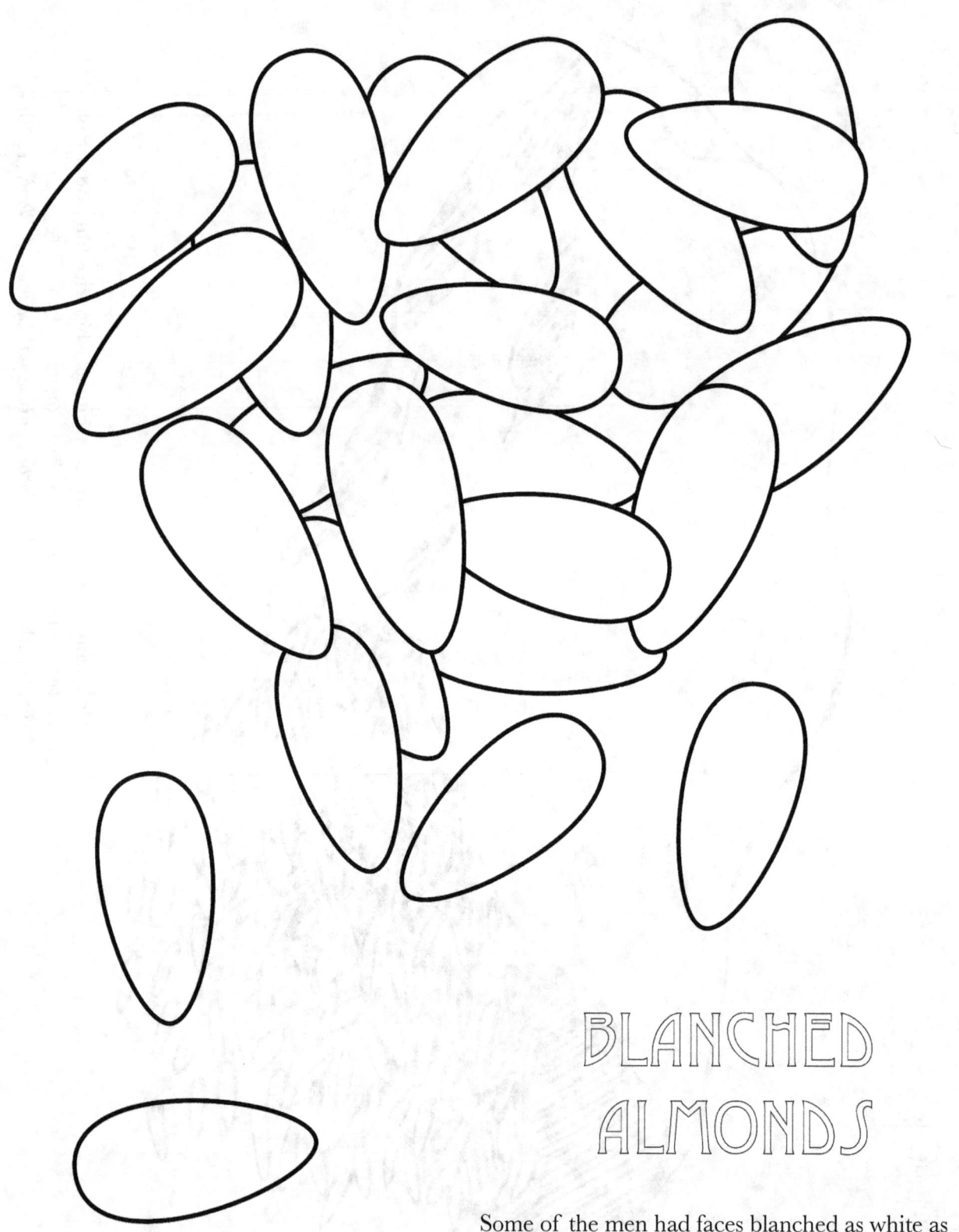

BLANCHED
ALMONDS

Some of the men had faces blanched as white as almonds and their eyes bulged out like billiard balls.
—Florence Lee Mallinson, *My Travels and Adventures in Alaska* (1914)

EASTER LILIES

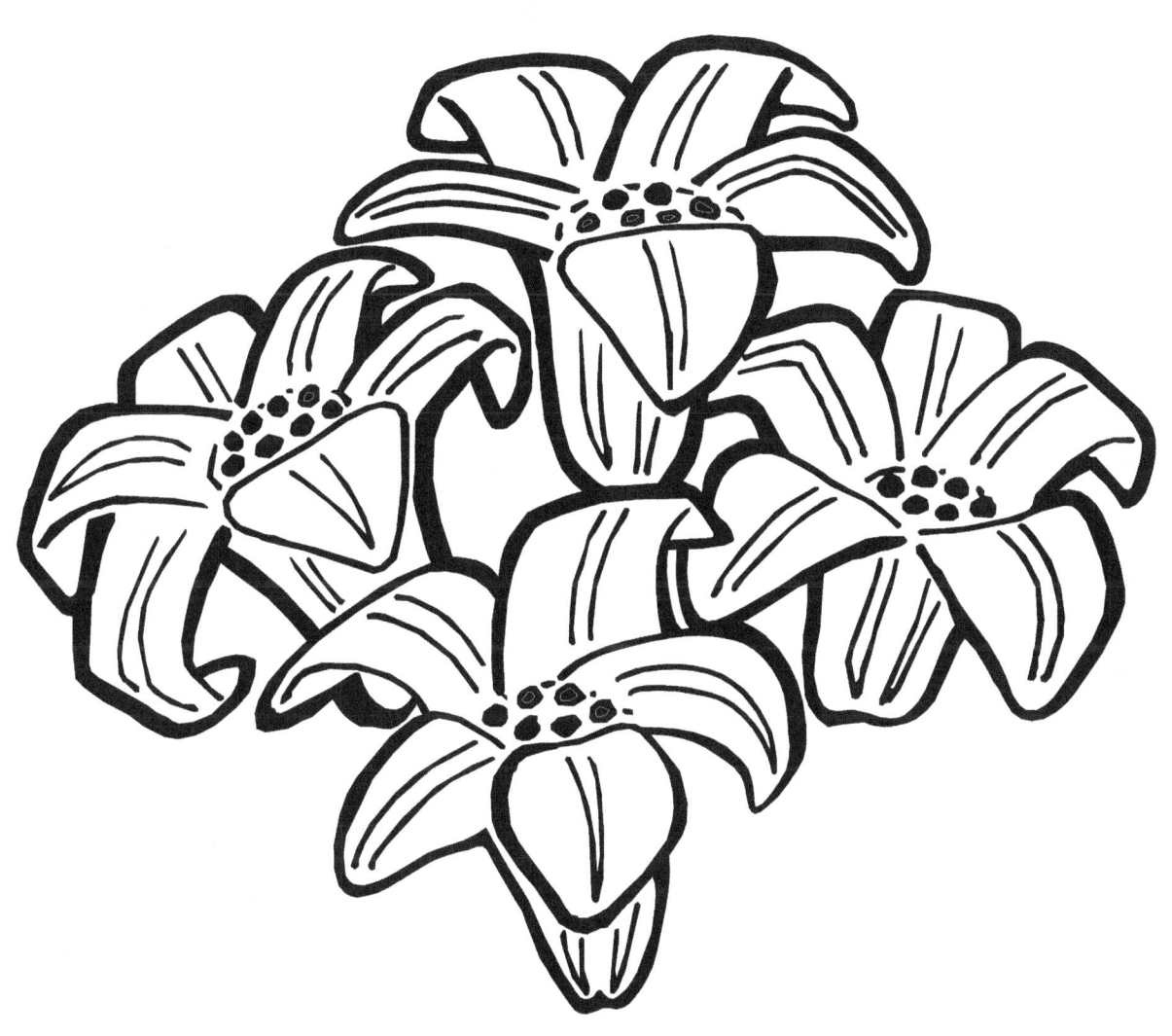

As white as a lily glimmered she
Like a ship's fair ghost upon the sea.
—D. G. Rossetti, "The White Ship" (1881)

MARSHMALLOW

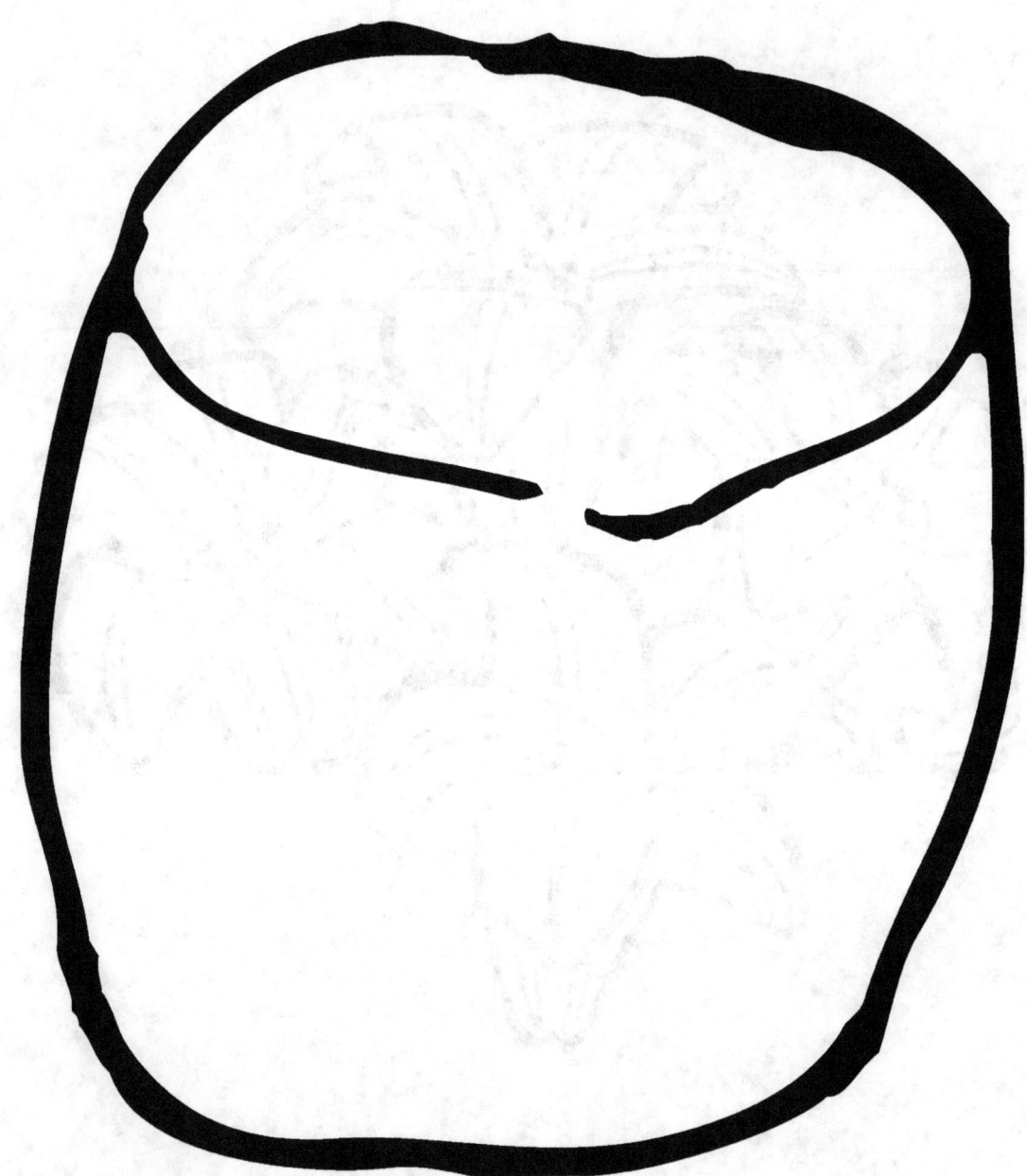

The bishop's robe was as white as marshmallow creme, and
flowed to the ground in front of me, so close that I could touch it.
—Robert T. Sharp, *No Dogs in Heaven* (2005)

ANDY WARHOL

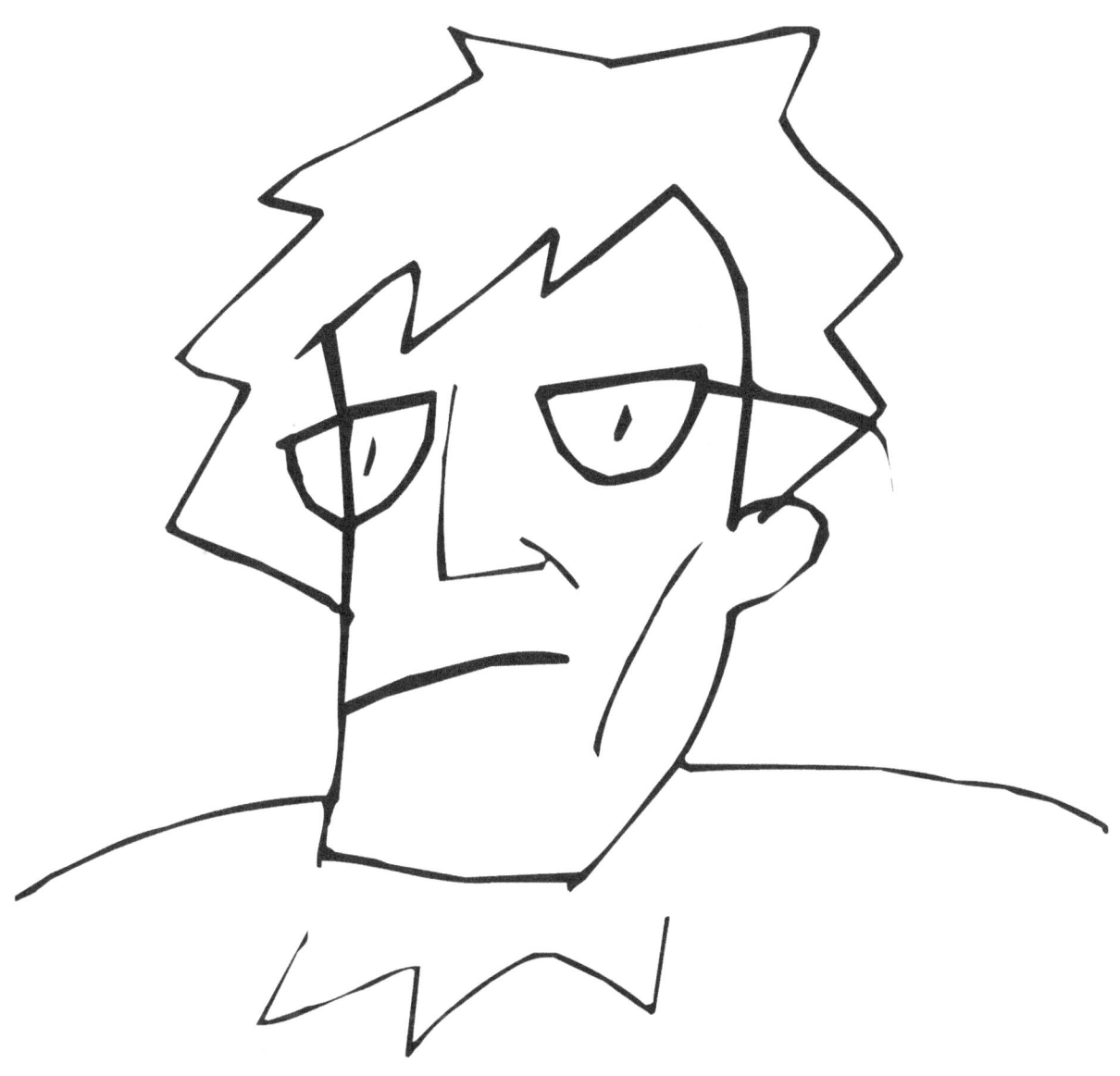

Or the whiteness of virtuous witchery; aerogram and
smoke signal, their billows white as Warhol.
—Bruce Olds, *Bucking the Tiger* (2002)

BUCKSKIN

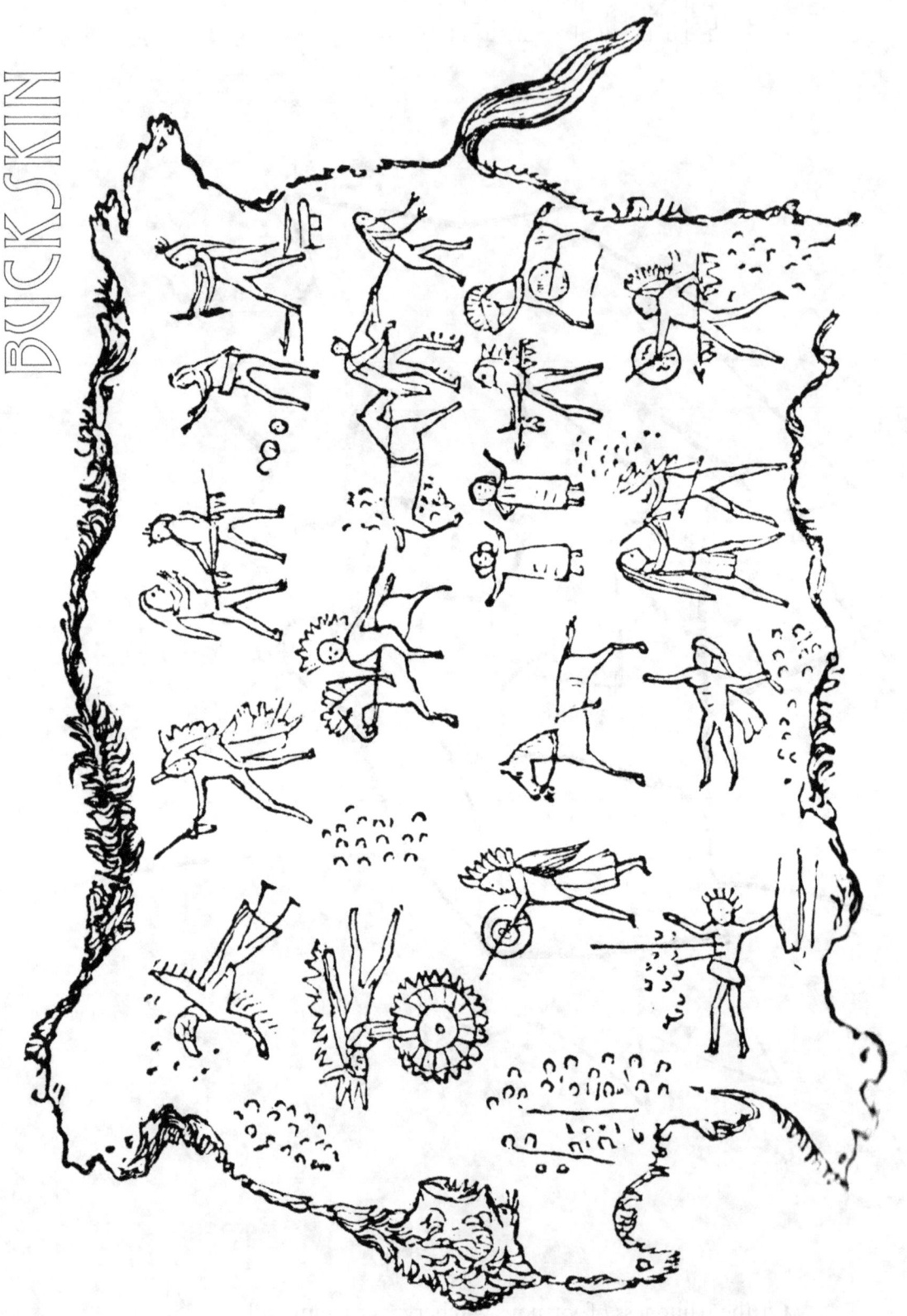

A buckskin, dressed and made as white as it can be made, goes over the shoulders and fastens around the neck and hangs down covering the back.

—Lucy Thompson, *To the American Indian* (1991)

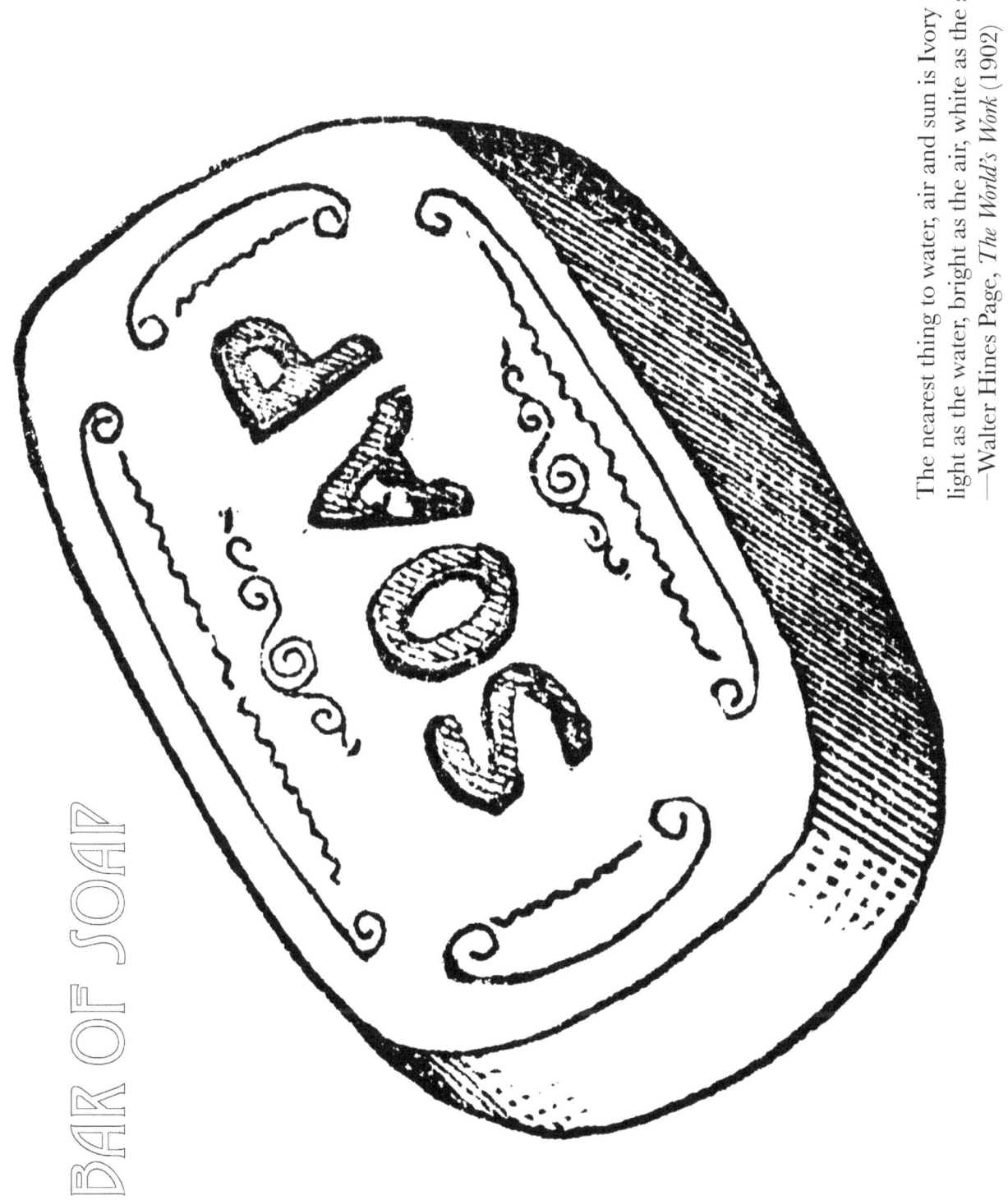

BAR OF SOAP

The nearest thing to water, air and sun is Ivory Soap:
light as the water, bright as the air, white as the sun.
—Walter Hines Page, *The World's Work* (1902)

SNEAKERS

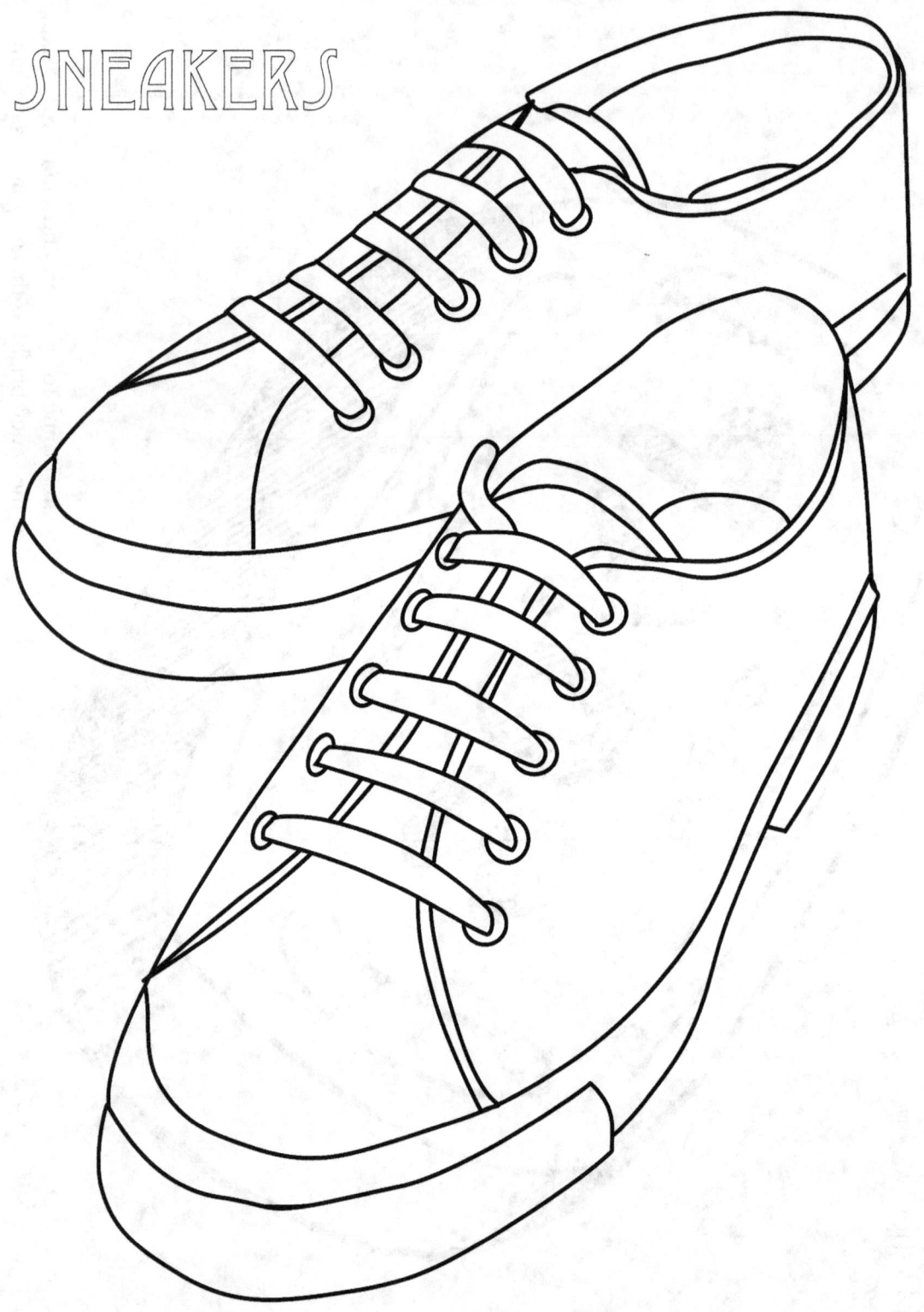

Her sneakers were just too damn white.
—Tom Perrotta, *Joe College* (2001)

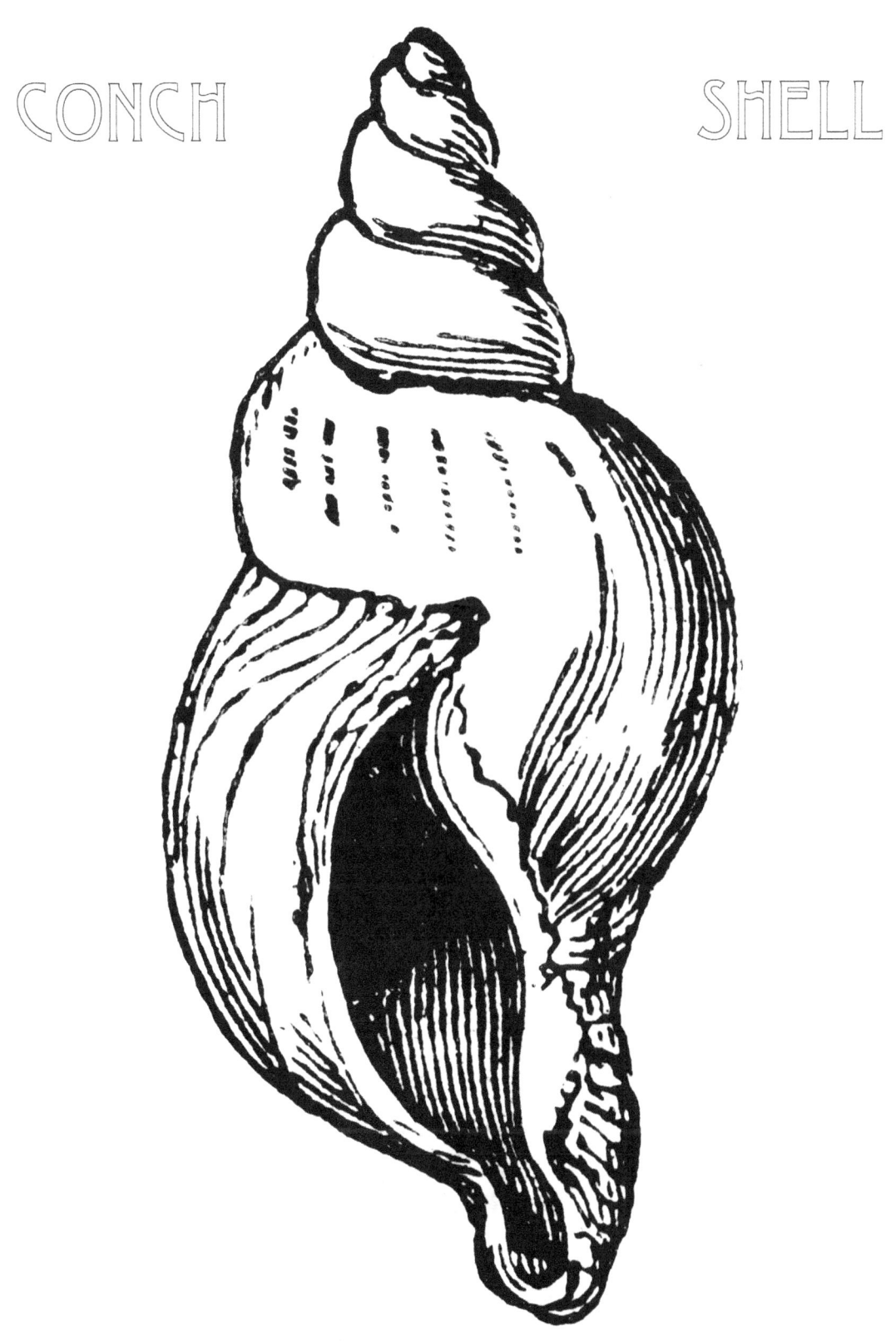

White as a conch shell, moonlike, proudly bearing
aloft the glorious coiled knot.
—Stephan V. Beyer, *The Cult of Tara* (1973)

SEAGULL

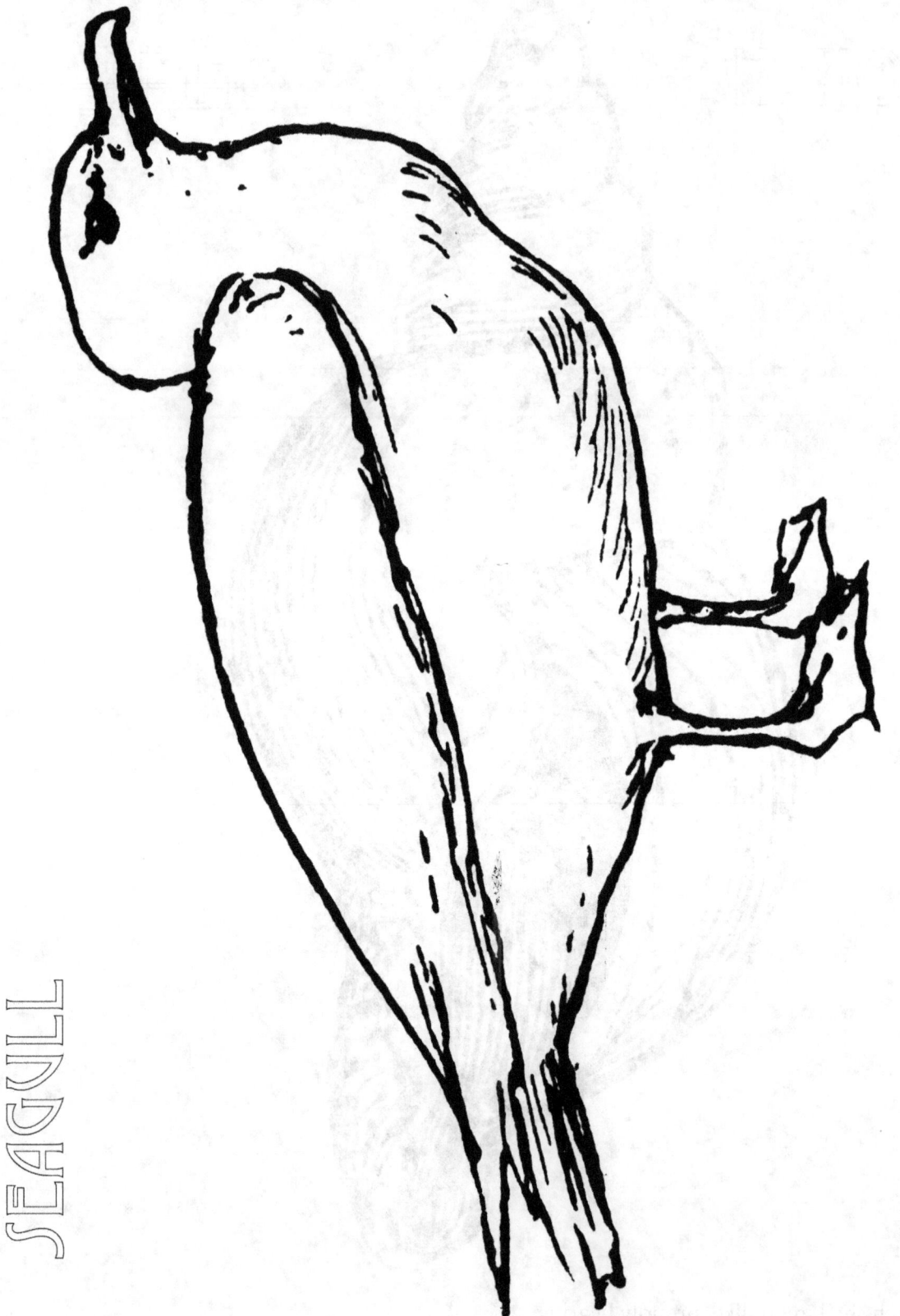

A wintry seagull hung white as a winter leaf above the surface of the waves.

—Achmat Dangor, *Waiting for Leila* (1981)

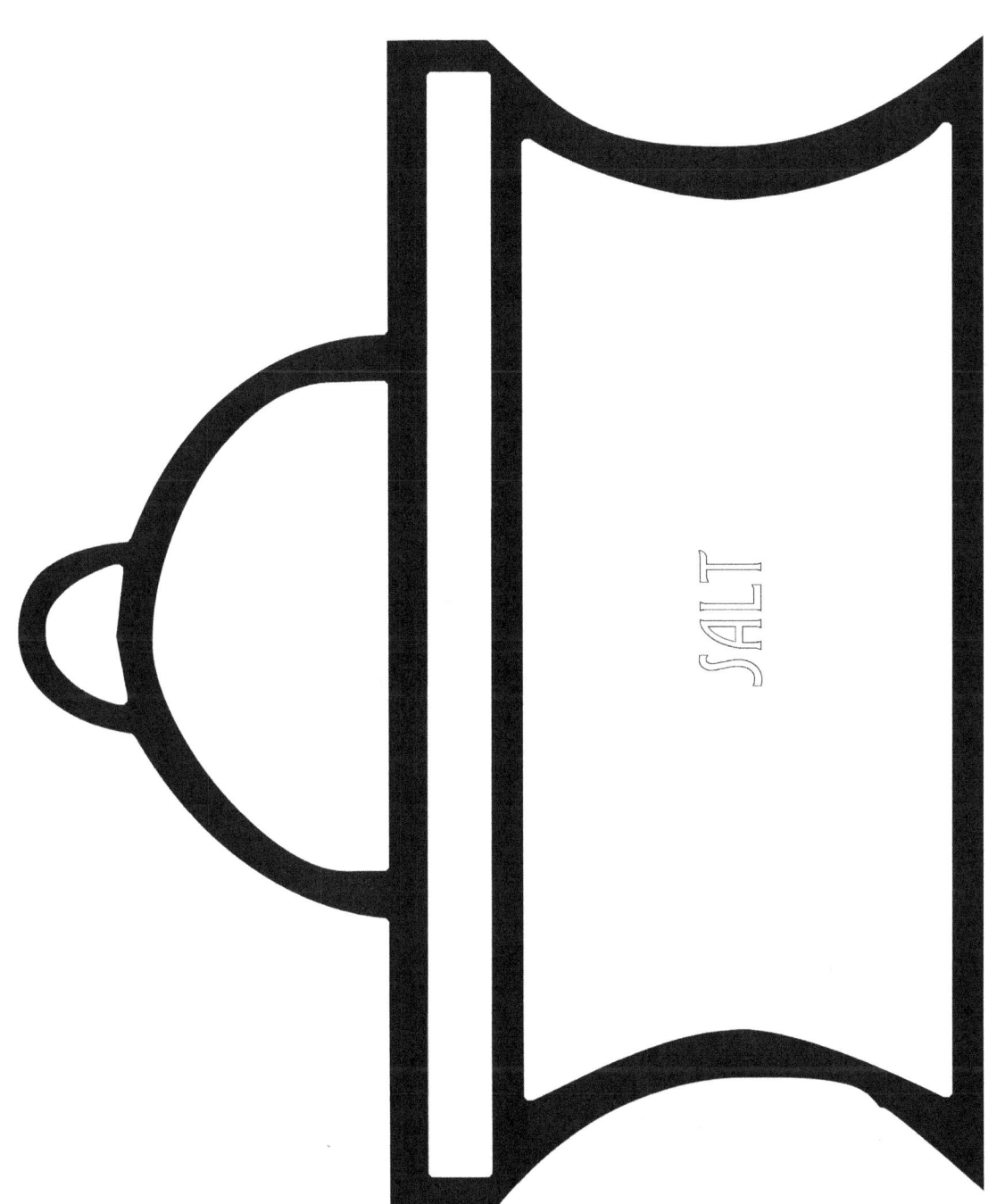

SALT

The salt glowed white as it showered down from her fist.
—Sarah Zettel, *The Usurper's Crown* (2003)

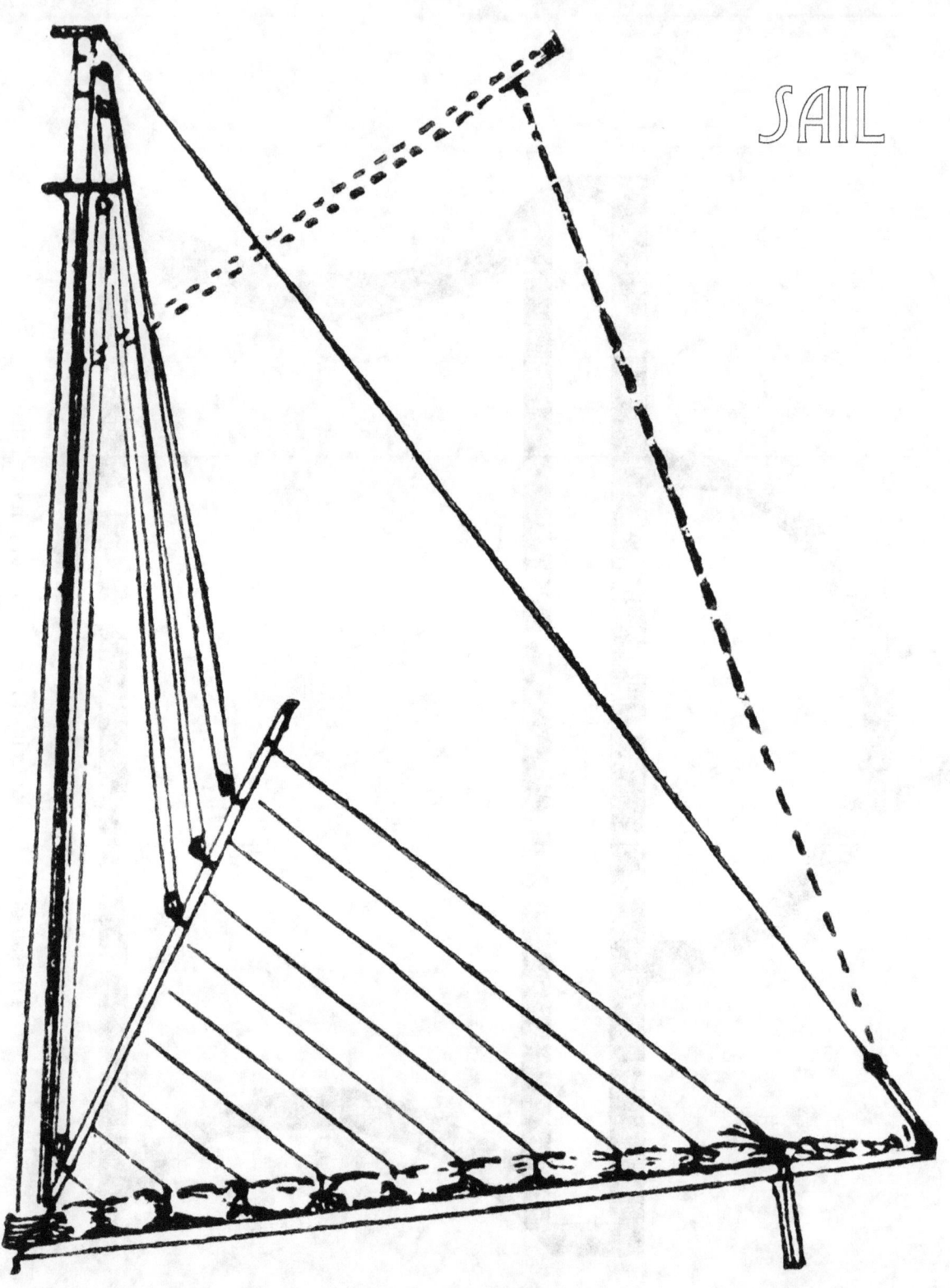

SAIL

White as the gleam of a receding sail.
—Henry Wadsworth Longfellow, "Holidays,"
A Book of Sonnets, Part II (1878)

THE BEATLES

Into a telephone, white as the White Album, she would
murmur the information that so-and-so was here.
—Philip Norman, *Shout!* (2005)